Australia's
Iron Lace

Australia's

Iron Lace

BRIAN TURNER

Line illustrations
by Robyn Fookes

GEORGE ALLEN & UNWIN
Sydney London Boston

First published in 1985
George Allen & Unwin Australia Pty Ltd
8 Napier Street, North Sydney, NSW 2060, Australia

George Allen & Unwin (Publishers) Ltd
Park Lane, Hemel Hempstead, Herts HP2 4TE, England

Allen & Unwin Inc
Fifty Cross Street, Winchester, Mass 01890, USA

National Library of Australia
Cataloguing-in-Publication entry:

Turner, Brian.
  Australia's iron lace.

  Bibliography.
  Includes index.
  ISBN 086861 481 5.

  1. Architectural ironwork, Australian—History—
  Pictorial works. 2. Architectural ironwork, Australian—
  Designs and plans—Pictorial works. 3. Decoration and
  ornament, Architectural—Australia—History—Pictorial
  works. 4. Ironwork—Australia—History—Pictorial
  works. I. Title.
739'.4794

Library of Congress Catalog Card Number: 84-71926

Designed by Pam Brewster

Typeset by Asco Trade Typesetters Ltd, Hong Kong

Printed by South China Printing Co., Hong Kong

Contents

Acknowledgements

This book could not have been completed without the help and encouragement of a large number of people. I am particularly indebted to Mr Bob Irving of the Graduate School of the Built Environment at the University of New South Wales who has been especially generous with his time and knowledge and made many useful suggestions and corrections to my manuscript.

Mr David Walster of Junee, New South Wales was equally generous with his knowledge. His family has operated a foundry and engineering firm in Junee since 1893 which supplied most of the Riverina with its cast iron decoration. I have drawn heavily on his knowledge and experience.

I would also like to thank the librarians of the Mitchell Library, Sydney, the John Oxley Library, Brisbane, the Australian National Library, Canberra, the Battye Library, Perth, The South Australian Collection of the Library of South Australia, the Allport Library and Museum of Fine Arts, Hobart, and the State Library of Victoria, Melbourne for their valuable assistance which was so cheerfully given.

I am also indebted to: Michael Campbell, Neil Champion, Bob Daniels, Reg Fookes, Stewart Game, Dorothy Gibson-Wilde, Gary Gillis, Leona Goldstein, Owen Hasemer, Max Kelly, Rae Lockey, B. 'Mack' Macgregor, Ian Molyneux, Catherine Snowdon, Ian Sperritt, Geoffrey Stilwell, John Storey, Barbara Valentine, John Wright.

This book could not have been written without the generosity of the Literature Board of the Australia Council in providing a special purpose grant to help subsidise the expenses of the 30 000 kilometres of travel which were involved in its research and photography.

Introduction

This book seeks to demonstrate the character of Australia's iron lace heritage. It is not intended as a panel by panel catalogue of all the forms of iron lace that have been used on Australia's buildings, but serves rather to portray the exuberance and vitality in its variations that can be seen from Cooktown to Hobart and from Balmain to Broome.

Cast iron decoration is older than the white history of Australia but it has left an impression on our architecture in a form that is uniquely Australian. Iron lace terraces and country pub verandahs are immensely popular with overseas visitors and tourist buses now cruise down the streets of revitalised areas such as Paddington in Sydney. Paradoxically, Australia's iron lace has spent most of its life unloved. It was abominated by contemporary architects as well as innovators such as William Morris who swam against the stream of Victorian convention.

During the first half of this century, those who lived in the iron lace terraces did not seem to have any special affection for it. In the 1950s New Orleans became popular with American and European tourists who flocked there to admire its decorative iron work. At the same time house owners in Sydney, Melbourne and Australian country towns were busy tearing down similar ironwork, or enclosing it with fibro or plywood in a frenzy to 'modernise'. They are now equally frenzied in their determination to put it back, often upside down, or simply using aluminium replicas. Examples of iron lace balustrades that have survived seem to have done so from an indifferent toleration of it rather than a conscious effort to preserve it.

Iron lace was a fashion, and, like all fashions, it had its ups and downs. In its heyday it was used most lavishly of all on terrace houses. These terrace house areas were also fashionable for a brief period and then degenerated into slums. They have now re-emerged as Australia's unique terrace house streets, expensively renovated and protected by Heritage Council listings. The rise, decline and revival of these areas is also a part of this story.

Cast iron is often mistakenly referred to as wrought iron. Cast iron panels were made by pouring the molten metal into moulds of the desired

A pair of English wrought iron gates from Chichester Cathedral.

A French wrought iron balcony, c. 1700, in the Victoria and Albert Museum.

A French wrought iron balcony front from the second half of the eighteenth century.

form. Cast iron contains more carbon than wrought iron; it is non-malleable when hot and brittle when cold and, unlike wrought iron, it cannot be hammered into any shape. Repetitive panels of the identical shape can be cast from the one pattern, whereas wrought iron was handcrafted and required superior artistry and skill. The foundries of the industrial revolution replaced the handcrafted skill of the smiths but inherited many of their traditional designs.

The wrought ironwork of medieval craftsmen can still be seen in Europe's churches and cathedrals. The finely worked grilles were riveted together to form screens around an interior chapel or tomb.

The art and design of the medieval smith was secondary to the artist and illuminator. His iron grille work followed the flourishes, curves and twists of the quill of the medieval calligrapher and illuminator on the parchment and vellum manuscripts of the middle ages. The long curling tendrils of the thirteenth century wrought iron door mountings found at Notre Dame cathedral in Paris have the same flourishes as the rubricated capitals in the pages of a medieval bible.

During the renaissance wrought iron grilles were used as security screens on the lower windows of the houses of the rich, from towns in Belgium to Florence in Italy. Another popular use for decorative wrought iron was as a canopy over a public well in the town square.

Otto Hoever, in his *Handbook of Wrought Iron* (London 1962), states that many of the masterpieces of the medieval and Renaissance smiths were lost when, during troubled and violent times, the ironwork was rehammered into weapons—an ironic reversal of turning swords into ploughshares.

In France, during the age of Louis XIV, wrought iron fences and grilles enclosed the chateaux of the nobility, making them secure as well as decorative. The iron gates on the forecourt of the sun king's palace at Versailles features a medallion of the sun as its central motif, but the tops of the railings were sharply spiked. Like modern barbed wire the sun king's enclosure was transparent and sharp, but at a later date proved incapable of withstanding the press of the mob.

In the early eighteenth century, a method of smelting iron using coke as fuel instead of charcoal, which was dependent on the ever diminishing supply of timber, was discovered. Cast iron was then used more widely and contributed to the progress of the industrial revolution, as its cheapness gradually caused it to usurp the place of wrought iron in architectural decoration. Both wrought and cast iron were used on London's Georgian era houses and its memory was still in the minds of Phillip and his exiles when they arrived at Sydney Cove in 1788.

No attempt at the study of iron lace can be made without constant reference to the books of the late Dr E. Graeme Robertson. Besides following his medical career as Melbourne's leading neurologist he somehow found time to write five books on iron lace. These pioneered the identification of patterns from old catalogues and records of those which were registered for patent. In his native Melbourne, few iron lace patterns escaped his eagle eye. Most of his books are now out of print although they can usually be found in libraries.

His earlier books were written over twenty years ago and many of his photographs now have a vintage appearance. Sadly, some of the buildings have been demolished, and other pictures show decrepit and slum-like streets in areas such as Sydney's Paddington, with sagging balconies of rusting iron, before the millions of dollars were spent by homeowners on restoration.

My most grateful acknowledgement goes to those individuals and groups whose enthusiasm and expenditure have resulted in the restoration of what is one of Australia's most distinctive architectural features.

I have tried to illustrate examples of Australia's rarest as well as most common and typical uses of iron lace and its patterns. No attempt has ever been made to record every cast iron baluster, ventilation grille and grave railing that was manufactured or used in this continent. To do so, a delightful but lengthy project would require more time and money than I have at my disposal. I can only apologise for the omission of any design that has been overlooked or remains undiscovered. Anyone fortunate enough to possess or to have observed one is welcome to submit it for future inclusion.

1

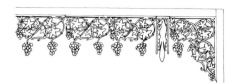

Beginnings

An illustration from the *Diderot Pictorial Encyclopedia of Trades and Industry* 1763, shows molten iron being ladled into two mould boxes (left) and into moulds embedded in the foundry floor. The two boys are skimming off slag.

His Excellency's house is composed of the common and Attic orders ... but ... it is simple and without any embellishment whatever.

Convict artist Thomas Watling on Governor Phillip's Government House.

Captain James Cook RN made two major mistakes in his otherwise brilliant naval career. One was to underestimate the temper of the natives of Hawaii which resulted in his death. The other was to pass by and not enter Sydney Harbour. Cook had seen and explored many magnificent natural waterways during his career but he missed the jewel of them all. Sailing past the sandstone bluffs of North and South Heads at a distance of four kilometres, as Cook did, it is possible to get an idea of the breadth of its interior. Cook elected not to enter. He noted a bay 'wherein there appeared to be a safe anchorage' and continued north, naming the harbour Port Jackson after an acquaintance, Sir George Jackson, one of the secretaries of the British Admiralty.

Eighteen years later, after a magnificent feat of navigation which brought his ragged First Fleet half way around the globe, Captain Arthur Phillip sailed into Port Jackson to establish his colony on the shores of Sydney Cove. His selection owed more to good luck than careful exploration.

The First Fleet had earlier arrived at Botany Bay, Cook's landing place during his voyage on the *Endeavour*. Disappointed at the shallowness of Botany Bay and its surrounding swamps and sandy soil, Phillip made an exploratory voyage three leagues to the north to examine the bay marked on Cook's map.

On a gentle and mild day, Phillip and a party of officers and marines sailed in three open boats out of Botany Bay and northwards past the coastline of rocky cliffs and beaches. From the shore groups of Aborigines shouted 'Warra, warra, warra,' which was interpreted as being neither expressions of welcome nor an invitation to land. As they sailed past the fierce cliffs on the southern side of the entrance to Cook's bay, Phillip was

Hand wrought balcony railings such as these were the forerunners of cast iron panels: above left from the palace of Marchese Castiglione in Milan and below left, from a building in St Marks Square, Venice. Both are sixteenth century.

not encouraged and expected to find it as uninspiring as Cook had marked it on his map. Rounding the southern headland he was astonished and delighted at the expanse of the harbour and later on finding a plentiful supply of fresh water.

He decided to found 'his government' beside a deep cove with 'the finest spring of water' flowing into it. He named it Sydney Cove, after Lord Sydney, Secretary of State, to whom Phillip was required to address his dispatches.

It was now eight months and two weeks since the fleet of eleven ships, to the relief of the citizens of Portsmouth, weighed anchor and sailed out of their harbour and down the Channel. Phillip then ordered his ships to complete the shortest and last leg of their long voyage and sail up to Port Jackson. Six days after their arrival at Botany Bay their chains rattled and anchors splashed down in Sydney Cove, close to the rocky shore with strange and beautifully coloured birds in the giant gum trees crowding down to the water's edge.

The disappointment of Botany Bay must have been the most dreadful setback for Phillip. During the voyage he and his officers were confident that Botany Bay was ideally suitable for a settlement. Cook had encouraged such optimism when he wrote 'instead of sand I found in many places a deep black soil, which we thought was capable of producing any kind of grain. At present it produceth, besides timber, as fine meadow as ever was seen'.

Sailing past the cliff which had hidden the expanse of Sydney Harbour from Cook's view, Phillip must have been desperately anxious for the fate of his colony in a land as unpromising as Botany Bay. His delight and surprise on entering Sydney Harbour is one of the pleasantest recorded moments in Australian history.

The raw materials and the conditions at Sydney Cove—the strange trees with a hardness never encountered before—would have tried the resources of skilled builders, had there been any. After scanning the lists of convicts, Phillip found only one brickmaker, Charles Bloodsworth, and twelve carpenters; the ships provided a further twelve.

The tools provided by the Admiralty soon proved to be of such an inferior quality that they blunted and warped on the hard eucalyptus. The human material, the convicts, who had been sentenced to hard work as well as banishment, proved to be as intractable as the local timber. The lashings and hangings which commenced soon after the landing failed to turn the pickpockets, forgers and thieves into empire builders, or to engender any enthusiasm for the toil of pioneering. Canvas tents were Australia's first European structures and work started urgently on building more permanent shelter as soon as the convicts were landed.

The convicts and carpenters toiled to build what has been called 'wattle and daub' huts, thatched with reeds from what is now known as Rushcutters Bay. The slab-sided walls were filled with clay to keep out the wind and rain and then a render of pipe clay was applied, or a coating of whitewash of lime which was made by burning the middens of heaped shells found on the camp grounds of the Aborigines on the harbour foreshores.

The reed and grass roofing soon dried out and proved to be entirely unsatisfactory. Artists in the First Fleet illustrated the Aborigines in canoes and beside their 'gunyahs', both made from stringybark, but either

There was no class consciousness in the use of cast iron decoration in nineteenth century Australia. It was used on grandiose mansions as well as Sydney's tiniest house. Number 43½ Edgeware Road, Marrickville, has a frontage of only three metres but carries a full panoply of ironwork.

the First Fleeters were slow to recognise its value, or else the Aborigines were reluctant to show them the skills required in removing it intact from the trees and flattening it with heat. Colonial artists and nineteenth century photographers such as Holtermann and Kerry have shown us that stringy-bark roofs covered most Australian pioneer homesteads, and structures in gold rush towns were covered with little else. During Australia's centenary in 1888 an attempt was made to find traces of some of these earliest habitations, but although there were still plenty of convict shacks in the Rocks area, only a few posts of doubtful origin were unearthed.

Convicts were moulding bricks only three months after the First Fleet dropped anchor, and by July 1788, only six months after its arrival, work was sufficiently completed on the Governor's residence for an inspection. The Aborigines expressed astonishment only at the staircase which allowed others to walk above their heads. In a letter home, the convict artist Thomas Watling rather unfairly carped at the lack of embellishment. Phillip's house was an imitation of a two-storey townhouse of Georgian London with glass windows that Phillip had the foresight to bring with him. He had originally planned on building his house on the western side of the cove, overlooking what is now Darling Harbour, but his second-in-command, the prickly Major Ross, had disputed his claim for the site, so in a simple ceremony in May 1788 Phillip laid the foundation-stone of his government house on the eastern side of the cove. The exact location of Phillip's house was uncertain until 1899, when a group of workmen uncovered his foundation stone on the south west corner of Phillip and Bridge Streets. At the time of writing, within a few years of Australia's bicentenary, the site is once again the subject of a dispute between developers and conservationists.

After travelling half way around the world from the crowded cities of Britain to the shores of a vast continent, the tiny settlement confined itself to a little more than a square kilometre around Sydney Cove. It was not only the fear of a massed attack by the Aborigines and the limited water resources of the Tank Stream which governed their behaviour and planning. Everything they encountered in Australia was in such bizarre contrast to England and their experience that it was more like landing on a new planet than a new continent. The trees shed bark rather than leaves, there was no English twilight, and instead of polite pattering English rain, torrential buckets full fell in the middle of a blazing hot summer.

An invisible umbilical cord of conditioning and nostalgia linked all planning and building to the English home model. Nor did it break free from it quickly. A hundred years later terrace houses were still being built in Australian cities with a parapet made obligatory as a fire protection requirement following the Great Fire of London in 1666.

Phillip's early plans for the controlled development of Sydney's streets were soon disregarded, even during the first few years of the settlement. The struggle for survival and the threat of starvation after repeated crop failures were uppermost in people's minds, not town planning.

When Phillip, his health broken, returned to England in 1792, his tiny colony still had the aspect of a military punishment camp with few substantial buildings. The avarice and greed of the officers of the New South Wales Corps dominated the colony till the arrival of Governor Macquarie in 1810. It is unlikely that any thoughts of a future national identity ever entered their minds; rum was their currency and land the premium commodity. Perhaps the activities of these early land sharks combined with Macquarie's system of land grants to emancipated convicts sowed the seeds of the obsessive Australian preoccupation with real estate and home ownership. Any Balmain or South Yarra dinner party is prefaced with conversation on house finance and land values—'do you rent or have you purchased?'. Governor Lachlan Macquarie arrived on the last day of 1809, bringing with him his own loyal regiment to replace the New South Wales Corp, and Mrs Macquarie and her small library of books on architecture. In the 22 years since the first tents were erected under the gum trees around Sydney Cove, Sydney had acquired some appalling squalor in the shacks along the undrained alleys of the Rocks area as well as some more ambitious dwellings of the merchant and officer classes.

The first glimmer of an Australian vernacular emerged in Captain John Macarthur's farmhouse at Parramatta which he and his wife Elizabeth moved into in 1794. The land further up the Parramatta river was found to be much more suitable for agriculture than at Sydney Cove, and Macarthur built a verandah on the northern aspect of his house overlooking the river on his 250 acre grant. Another verandah was added on the eastern side, around 1806. A wide verandah was probably adapted from those seen on British colonial buildings in India and the West Indies and it was to emerge as one of the most distinctive features of Australian homesteads and country towns. The openwork cast iron columns seen on Elizabeth Farm today are a later addition.

Macquarie was quick to tour his domain and one of his first requests to London was for an architect to draw the plans for his vision of ordered barracks, inns, hospitals, churches and a lighthouse that he had in his mind. It was Francis Greenway's skill with a pen which prompted his transportation to New South Wales as a convict on board the *General Hewitt*. He arrived in February 1814 to serve his fourteen year sentence for forgery. Parsimonious Whitehall had refused Macquarie's request for an architect, but Francis Greenway arrived with a letter of recommendation, describing him as 'an architect of merit'.

Apart from being a familiar face on the $10 note, Greenway's name is known as a colonial architect to Australians who know the name of no other. It is common to call buildings of his design, and sometimes a few which are not, with the added apellation of his name. The temperamental and tactless architect was granted his emancipation within three years, and as Macquarie's official civil architect he designed a prodigious number of buildings and supervised the erection of many of them. His barracks, churches, a lighthouse and other government buildings were not just a transplant of the harmonious and balanced Georgian proportions from his former professional practice in Bristol; each bears the stamp of his individual touch, and contributes to what is regarded as Australia's finest architectural heritage.

Greenway later quarrelled with Macquarie, as he did with everyone else, and both were brought down by lesser men, but not before they had lifted the standards of construction and design which the growing prosperity of the colony could now afford.

Wagon loads of wool were now trundling in from the road across the Blue Mountains and from pastures on the southern highlands. Warehouses for the bales of wool and handsome two-storey homes for the merchants and successful emancipists were now appearing, as well as shops for the

Conrad Martins made this preliminary sketch for a watercolour of Regentville, near Penrith, in 1835—unfortunately he did not clarify the pattern on the balcony railing. This early colonial mansion was destroyed by fire in the 1860s. (*Mitchell Library*)

refinements they could now afford. A generation of locally born 'currency lads and lasses' had come to maturity and though they may not have firmly identified themselves as being Australian, they would raise their glasses to 'Boys—to the land we live in'.

On a fine morning in 1836, before 'a light morning air', the ten-gun brig *Beagle* rounded the south head of Sydney Harbour and dropped anchor in Sydney Cove. That evening the *Beagle's* unpaid naturalist, Charles Darwin, went for a stroll through the town. Young Charles was considering becoming a clergyman, but instead he joined the *Beagle* on its world cruise of scientific research during which the future author of *The Origin of the Species* hoped he would find scientific evidence of the literal truth of the bible, especially the book of Genesis.

No newspaper reported the visit of one of the greatest minds of the nineteenth century but some of the locals must have found time to pause and chat to the polite and curious young naturalist from the *Beagle*. As he recorded in his journal, the conversation, then as now, generally turned to real estate. 'The number of houses and other buildings just finished was truly surprising; nevertheless, every one complained of the high rents and the difficulty in procuring a house.'

On his return from a brief excursion across the Blue Mountains to Bathurst Charles was invited to lunch at a homestead a short distance outside Sydney. At the table he was pleased to find himself among a bevy of young colonial beauties. He asked one sitting next to him whether she missed England. 'Oh' she replied, 'we are Australian and know nothing of England'. Perhaps the great scientist was being teased but the remark

Wynyard Terrace in Carrington Street was a fashionable address in 1850s Sydney. This photograph was taken just prior to its demolition in 1923—however, the last tenant whose feet can be seen propped up on the balcony does not seem to be unduly worried. The baluster panels were probably imported, the wider one (beneath the pair of feet) has disappeared altogether, though it must have been around in 1954 when Morton Herman published his sketch of it in his book '*The Early Australian Architects and their Work*'. The narrow one has only been seen once, on 'Margaretta Cottage', 6 Leichhardt Street, Glebe, on a verandah which was added to the older sandstone house in the 1850s. (*City of Sydney Council*)

'Margaretta Cottage', Glebe.

This stereograph of George Street was taken in the mid-1850s. The cantilever balcony on David Jones & Co. store, above the top-hatted coachman, has a wrought or cast iron railing. The accuracy of Joseph Fowles' line drawings can be seen by comparing the photograph with an enlargement of his illustration from *Sydney in 1848*.

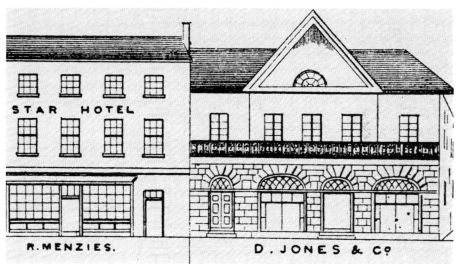

seems to have taken him aback. Darwin, British to his boot-straps, imagined that all colonials considered themselves to be transplanted Englishmen and he reported the conversation in a letter to his family in England.

In 1847, an unkind art critic of the *Sydney Morning Herald* after viewing some paintings of the marine artist Joseph Fowles, claimed that the young artist still had 'too much green in his eye'. The green notwithstanding, Joseph Fowles had a fine draughtsman's eye, and between 1848 and 1850 he issued in twenty parts his extraordinary copper plate engravings and descriptive text of *Sydney in 1848*. Fowles' meticulous eye and pen drew strips of elevated plans of the streets of Sydney and his quaint prose, with its extraordinary punctuation, accompanies the reader on a social as well as an architectural tour of his 'metropolis of Australia'. The market he had in mind for his publication comprised colonists who would send his engravings back to England to impress relatives and friends with the prosperity of their new life. It is a pity Fowles' survey did not extend past Bridge Street and into the bawdy Rocks area to leave us with a record of the other side of Sydney life, but for the purposes of the book Fowles swept the Rocks area 'under the carpet'. He preferred to draw churches:

> to shew that the Colonists have not been inattentive to matters of higher import, we shall display to our Readers the beautiful and commodious Buildings raised by piety and industry for the use of Religion.[1]

Opposite Two survivors of Horbury Terrace (c. 1836), the 'heart and honeysuckle' pattern on the window guards is commonly seen in London (see page 27) and *below* Joseph Fowles' Horbury Terrace 'the private residence of many respectable families', from his *Sydney in 1848*.

Fowles' drawings show us the streets of a prosperous, large town of elegant two- and three-storey Georgian houses and shop terraces. At least 57 have what is either cast or wrought iron balustrades on their balconies or verandahs. Some are shown as a plain crisscross pattern which could be either wrought or cast or even a wooden lattice. This is probably the same as or similar to the ironwork shown in the photograph of Wynyard Terrace which was old when the picture was taken before its demolition in 1923 (see page 18).

Another of Fowles' illustrations shows the David Jones and Co. store on the corner of George and Barrack Streets. In the stereograph, taken only six years after Fowles published his book, the David Jones store and its cast iron balcony can be seen on the left hand side, with a top-hatted coachman waiting patiently outside on the unpaved street. Other horses and canvas awnings can be seen further down George Street. The state of the road contrasts with the elegant and prosperous looking architecture (see page 19).

A tour through Fowles' book shows several buildings with another import from Georgian London as well as iron balustraded balconies. Balconettes appear in front of some of the high windows—these miniature iron balconies with a grating floor project only about 300 mm with a short railing height of 150–450 mm, and are thought to be partly decorative and partly functional, providing a safe seat for cleaning windows.

Two happy survivors of the 1840s streets that Fowles drew so faithfully in his wonderful record of Sydney can still be seen today. Two double-storey houses of the original seven that comprised Horbury Terrace, 'the private residence of many respectable families', still stand at 171 and 173 Macquarie Street. Number 173 (the left) has undergone several facelifts but has now been restored to match its twin on the right. An examination with a magnifying glass of Fowles' illustration shows that number 171 is in its original state and has its original castings still intact. Number 173 has been restored, and after a search, original matching balconette panels were installed. This pattern is one of the most common

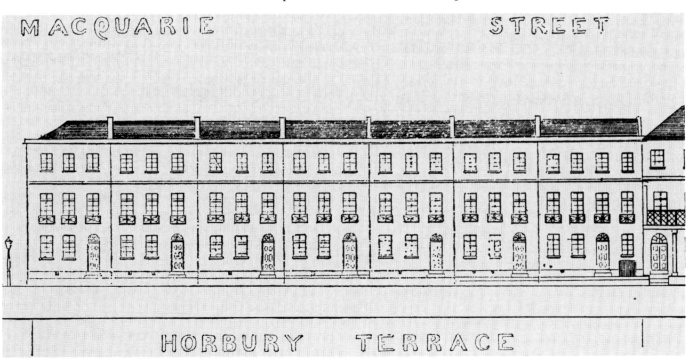

MACQUARIE STREET

HORBURY TERRACE

Opposite An elegant hand crafted transom grille of the Louis XVI period. The wrought and *repoussé* motifs of garlands and a quiver were made by a master craftsman in Brussels.

Right This fragment of an early thirteenth century choir screen was made into a fire screen during the eighteenth century. Its separate strips of wrought iron are bound together with metal collars.

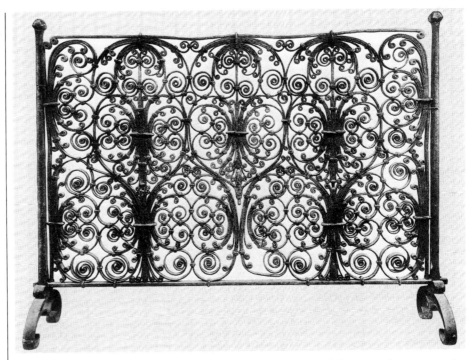

English patterns and can still be seen in London and frequently appears in old photographs of early Sydney buildings that have since been demolished. It is probably the earliest English pattern which was imported to Sydney but is now rare (see page 27).

Cast iron railings had already been in use for 74 years in England when Phillip and his fleet sailed into Botany Bay. In 1714 a cast iron fence was erected around St Paul's Cathedral in London. The wrought iron decoration on the wealthy Georgian townhouses of London must still have been fresh in the minds of the thieves, pickpockets and forgers, as the reason for their presence in the holds of the transports was their transgression against the savage British laws of property which protected the privileged classes who lived in them.

The Georgian era, which corresponded with the settlement at Sydney Cove, was an era of enlightened ideas—and institutional decay. It was a period of exquisite refinement of design and taste; book-bindings, furniture, clocks, fashions and architecture reached an apogee, maintained by a level of craftsmanship that has never been seen since. The elegance of the period also extended to ironwork, mostly wrought ironwork, which was the predecessor of the subject of this book, and cast ironwork—there should be no confusing the two.

Wrought iron is the older craft where the smith heated and then hammered the red hot iron into elegant, long, ribbon-like patterns. In France, three dimensional ornament was made by *repoussé*, that is, by hammering out a design from the reverse side. These were then used as a central motif in a baluster panel or gateway.

Some beautiful examples of medieval wrought iron have survived in the great cathedrals of Europe. Later, in the houses of the rich during the seventeenth and eighteenth centuries, it was fashionable to use a section of antique wrought iron as a firescreen in front of a fireplace. Iron is a material which has more associations with war than with art. Just as much of Europe's medieval wrought iron was rehammered into swords and other edged weapons during wartime, the people of London during two

The anthemion pattern, second row in a page of Cottingham's *Director*, was probably designed by Robert Adam. It was popular in eighteenth century London and was among the first to arrive in Sydney. The wide pattern, second row above right, was used in Tasmania. These pages are from a rare copy of L. N. Cottingham's *The Smith's, Founder's and Ornamental Metal Worker's Director*, London, no date, held in the TAFE Library, Sydney.

world wars were called upon to strip off the cast iron decoration from their houses and donate it as scrap to the war effort. Much of London's cast iron decoration went in this manner though a lot can still be seen in Brighton and the south of England. In riots in Liverpool during the depression an uprooted spiked iron railing was the traditional street fighter's weapon, much as the cobblestone has been in Paris.

Cast iron is not hand crafted but is made by pouring the molten metal into a mould of the desired shape and then cooled. The mould can only be used once but provided a master pattern is kept the process can be repeated as many times as desired, in much the same way as any number of photographs can be made from a negative.

Wrought iron is essentially a malleable material which can be hammered out into thin open and flowing designs. Cast iron, because of the nature of its brittleness and the method of reproduction, demands a heavier, more space filling and sculptured pattern. Cast iron is essentially a carving reproduced in iron. Cast iron is brittle and non-malleable but can withstand great superimposed weight, an ideal quality, as was found early in the industrial revolution, making it suitable for building columns and bridges.

The earliest dated objects of cast iron are small statues from sixth century China. Cast iron objects such as firebacks have also survived from the middle ages in Europe. The techniques of casting were known in Europe but that of firing a furnace with coke was not. Foundries were dependent on charcoal for their furnaces. In England it came from an ever diminishing supply of trees, and foundries often had to close until a further supply of charcoal could be accumulated.

England had, however, an abundance of coal, and around 1713 a Shropshire ironmaster, Abraham Darby, discovered a successful method of firing a furnace with coke up to the high temperatures required for smelting. Iron ore was placed between layers of coke, air was blown into the furnace and the molten iron collected in moulds below was called 'pig iron'. Darby's discovery at Coalbrookdale was later improved upon, the higher temperature coke fired furnaces made the remelting of pig iron and the development of castings much cheaper and more efficient—it also made the industrial revolution possible. Darby's Coalbrookdale foundry grew into the world's largest. Any members of the First Fleet from Shropshire would have seen the cast iron bridge across the Severn Gorge, built by a descendant of Darby's in 1781.

The craft of the smith was one of the first to be replaced by the new technology. Working under the directions of an architect, the smith would work on the building site and, with his hammer, anvil and bellows, would handcraft a gate, window guard or balustrade. The smith had to work swiftly while his iron remained red hot and relied on his eyes and hands to achieve the symmetry in metal that he had in his mind or in the sketch that he followed. The pattern he fashioned could be of the architect's or of his own design, or taken from any one of the pattern books which were available.

After the Battle of Waterloo (1815) the smith was gradually replaced on the building sites. Prefabricated cast iron panels, in designs copied from the same pattern books and often cast to imitate the finely hammered out wrought iron, began to arrive from Coalbrookdale and other foundries.

On 10 October 1823 Lewis Nockalls Cottingham, a London architect and antiquarian, published his *Ornamental Metal Workers Director*, a collection of ironwork patterns he had gathered from other pattern books and from copying existing work from other designers, a fact which the eloquent Cottingham acknowledges in his preface:

> many of the subjects introduced in this Work have been executed from the designs of the most eminent artists; and those composed by the Author are from the best specimens of antique ornament.[2]

An enlarged second edition, *The Smith and Founder's Director*, was published the following year and was the most influential pattern book in the rapidly expanding industry of decorative cast iron. From Cottingham's (1823) preface again:

> The great improvement that has taken place in our Brass and Iron Foundries within these last twenty years, has elevated this branch of English manufacture far above that of any other country, and raised the articles which were formerly considered as merely gross and ponderous, into the scale of ornamental embellishment in which utility and security are united with lightness and elegance of classical design.[3]

Not all architects and critics agreed with Cottingham on the elegance of cast iron and many regretted the upstart usurpation of the smith's craft by the arrival of the cheaper and artless mass-produced castings. John Ruskin was the most influential art critic of nineteenth-century England. In his book *The Seven Lamps of Architecture* published in 1849, he condemned cast iron as being neither light nor elegant. Ruskin believed that the merit of all decorative works was 'in proportion to the hand-work upon them'.

Above This cast iron balcony front is on display in the Victoria and Albert Museum, London, and was installed on 12 John Street, Adelphi, in about 1775, thirteen years before the settlement at Sydney Cove. (*Victoria and Albert Museum*) It is now rare in Sydney but appears in photographs of buildings long since demolished such as this, hotel in Redfern, above left. (*City of Sydney Council*)

Below left This balcony of old ironwork is in Crown Street, Woolloomooloo and has a red light above it. 'You can take a picture when the door's closed' said the lady in the doorway below.

Below These old terraces at 44 and 46 Darling Street, Balmain have the rare half and quarter panels in the same pattern.

The repetitiveness of cast iron made it 'cold, clumsy and vulgar... I believe no cause to have been more active in the degradation of our national feeling for beauty than the constant use of cast iron ornaments'.

Alternating pontifications, abuse and praise were heaped upon the use of cast iron decoration throughout its life from Wren to Ruskin. During its fashionable revival over the past 25 years such lights as Robin Boyd and Sir John Betjeman have added theirs, but none of its critics could deny the fact that this cheaper form of ironwork made it available to all who wished to use it.

Meanwhile, back in the prosperous and rumbustious town of Sydney, terraces, mansions and homesteads were being built with balconies and verandahs. 'The wide verandahs' remarks Fowles in *Sydney in 1848* 'afford a cool shelter from the heat of the meridian sun, and give the cottages an air of shady retirement, which has its own peculiar elegance'. One of the most popular of Cottingham's designs was the anthemion (honeysuckle) pattern shown on a page from his *Director* on page 24. It was popular in London and was exported to Sydney and can be seen on Horbury Terrace. It is now rare but one balcony can still be seen in Albion Street, Surry Hills and another in Crown Street, Woolloomooloo. Half and quarter panels were also made in this design to allow for variation in the length of a balustrade and these can be seen in a row of terraces at 44–48 Darling Street in Balmain.

Building fashions, though lagging some ten years behind, still tended to follow those of London and the colonists decorated their shady balconies and verandahs with cast iron panels. The remarkably clear photograph taken in the late 1850s is probably the oldest Sydney photograph where the iron lace pattern is clearly recognisable. The gate and panels are of a design which is still common in Sydney but rare in London; perhaps was among

Australia's Iron Lace

While taking this picture at his friends' place in Glebe in the late 1850s, Professor John Smith unintentionally focused his camera on the ironwork instead of his friends behind it and left us with what is probably the oldest Sydney photograph where the iron lace pattern is clearly recognisable. The same pattern was still being advertised in the 1914 Illustrated Catalogue of the "Sun" Foundry, Hindley Street, Adelaide, long after the heyday of cast iron decoration—it is extraordinary that any decorative design could remain fashionable for sixty years. The six open grille columns along the verandah show that they were being used in Sydney at this period though their popularity did not reach Melbourne. (*Sydney University Archives*)

the first patterns to be cast here. This early photograph also demonstrates that flat open columns were being used in Sydney at the time though their popularity was not repeated in Melbourne.

It is impossible to say exactly when the first cast iron panels were imported or when they were first manufactured here. An advertisement in the *Sydney Herald* (12 November 1835) offers 'Balcony railing, in panels of different patterns' and cast iron gates for sale. These were imported and just landed from the *William*.

It is a popular but incorrect notion among Australians that the cast iron on their houses was transported to Australia as ships' ballast. Robin Boyd's classic, *Australia's Home* (1952), is one of the most illuminating and entertaining books written on Australian architecture; but in an article appearing in the *Architectural Review* in 1956 he wrote that the fragile and brittle cast iron panels 'came packed in straw from England as convenient ballast deep in the holds of the light sailing ships'. One of the qualities of cast iron is that it can withstand great superimposed weight but its major failing is the ease with which a sharp lateral blow will shatter it. The 'cast iron panels and two pairs of gates advertised by the trader George Salt

The *William* arrived in Sydney Cove on 9 October 1835 and part of its cargo was domestic ironwork which was advertised in the *Sydney Herald* on 12 November 1835. There were, however, foundries operating in Sydney and Hobart at this time.

FOR SALE.

JUST LANDED, ex "WILLIAM,"

BALCONY RAILING, in panels, of different patterns

Area or Park Railings

Two pair of Cast Iron Gates

Iron Spouting, in lengths of six feet

Iron Wall Pipes, with heads and shoes complete, from two and a half to four inches in diameter

Cast Iron Sash Weights, from four to eight ℔s.

Hinges, Locks, Bolts, Latches, Screws, Manger Rings, Curtain Bands and Pins, Sash Fastenings, &c. &c.

Tinned Iron Saucepans and Stewpans, with covers

Saddles and Bridles

Musket, Gun, and Pistol Flints

Parker and Wyatt's, best Roman Cement

GEORGE SALT TUCKER.

James' Buildings, George-street,
7th November, 1835.

Tucker may well have been deep in the hold of the *William* but carefully stowed as fare-paying cargo and packed in wood.

The Battye Library in Perth holds the papers of Charles Harpur, a wealthy parliamentarian who built *Woodbridge*, a family mansion on the upper reaches of the Swan River. Harpur had the ironwork for *Woodbridge* imported from England; among his papers is the invoice from the Rotherham Foundry Company Limited in England dated 28 September 1883.

The total cost of 76 yards of balustrading, 44 round columns plus spandrils and brackets etc., as well as a spiral staircase and landing stairs amounted to £250. Equal space was given on the invoice to the elaborate packing details for 'foreign shipment', and though the 44 columns travelled loose, this amounted to a further £22.6.0. Even so a further four yards of balustrade was included as replacement 'in the event of breakage'. As this did not include the freight charges on 'SS *Kingdom of Saxony* for Swan River' the packing charges amounted to almost 10 per cent of the cost of the ironwork.

The appealing piece of folklore of iron lace panels travelling as ships' ballast probably had its origins in the practice of ballasting ships with pig iron ingots. Pig iron had not yet been successfully smelted in Australia on a commercial basis and was imported in vast amounts. This may then have been cast into iron lace panels at local foundries.

The ultimate cycle of fashion—broken nineteenth century iron lace panels are among the scrap iron at Grahame's Foundry to be reused in the furnace to cast a modern reproduction. The top box is placed on the lower one in which the panel to be recast is half embedded, the impression is thus formed between the two. A covering of the white 'parting powder' allows the two boxes to separate cleanly for the pattern to be removed. Mr Jack Thomas, having removed the panel seen behind him, checks its impression in the bottom box. Molten iron is poured into the mould within the two rejoined boxes and the new panel is removed twenty minutes later. The metal remaining in the pouring vents and the hole left for escaping steam and gases is snapped off with a sharp inward blow.

The first recorded foundry in Sydney is that of James Blanch who, in 1823, established a foundry and engineering shop next to the Royal Hotel in George Street. In an address to the Royal Society in 1900 on *A Hundred Years of Engineering*, Norman Selfe, a pioneer in engineering himself, stated that an old beam steam engine made by Blanch was still in existence in an old flour mill at Dapto on the south coast. The versatile Blanch advertised 'handsome dish covers, equal to any made in London' and though it is not known whether he cast any decorative ironwork, he also advertised 'umbrellas and parasols neatly repaired'.

Casting balustrade panels would have held no mysteries to the resourceful colonial engineers and the same method has not altered over the years. An imported panel could have been polished and treated for use as a pattern or, if the pattern was an original one, it would first have been hand carved in a straight-grained wood. A fragile wooden master panel would have had a short life in a foundry; it would inevitably be broken or burnt so a special fine casting in iron or bronze, which were not so fragile, and with its edges finely polished and filed, would have been used for forming the moulds once one was cast. The original wooden pattern would have hung safely on the wall if needed for future use.

I was fortunate enough to visit Grahame's Foundry in Newtown in Sydney, a foundry still using traditional methods, while a duplicate was being made of a century-old baluster panel that had been dropped and a few inches of its corner had broken off. As the owner of the foundry, Mr Owen Hasemer pointed out, more skill and time were involved in the making of the mould than in the brief but more spectacular process of pouring the molten metal into it.

Imagine two identical shallow metal boxes. One is rammed full of a mixture of moist black loam with a binding of clay, enough to bind together in a lump when a handful is squeezed. The iron panel is half embedded in the bottom box and a covering of 'parting powder' containing some asbestos is dusted over the top. The top box, also tightly rammed

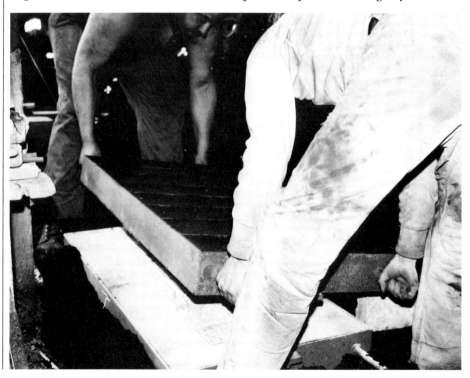

Curved panels of a flat design could be made by casting a panel in lead which could then be easily curved and a bronze master panel finally cast from it.

with the same mixture, is placed on top of the bottom box and receives the impression of the half exposed panel and the total impression of the pattern is thus formed within the two boxes. Holes are made in the top box to allow for pouring and for gases and steam to escape. The top box is removed, the dusting of 'parting powder' preventing the two layers from binding together. The iron panel is gently tapped to slightly enlarge the impression and to ease its removal. The broken and chipped parts of the damaged original are skilfully made good in the mould by the foundry foreman, Mr Jack Thomas, using special tools. The two boxes are rejoined, with the hollow impression of the new panel between them, and set aside with other moulds until the following day when the furnace will be fired and the molten metal poured.

On 'pouring day' a mixture of pig iron ingots and 10 per cent scrap iron is fed into the furnace and the liquid metal, plopping and splashing like soup from a cauldron, is poured into a container beneath it. This is poured into smaller crucibles, held at arm's length with carrying rods by the workmen, who carry it to the prepared moulds and carefully pour it in through the holes in the top box of the mould. Twenty minutes later the boxes are separated and the new panel, still hot and smoking, is removed, the moulding sand collapses and is hosed down and shovelled back with the new to be blended through and reused. The metal remaining from the pouring vents on the panel is snapped off with a sharp inward blow. 'People have been casting metal like this since Moses was a kid,' said Jack.

Curved and flat panels of the same design are not uncommon on terrace house balconies. These were made by casting a flat panel in lead which could be easily curved into the desired shape; a master panel was then cast in bronze from it. Casting curved panels required larger boxes and demanded skilful moulding.

Round hollow columns were also cast in the one piece from a master pattern whose impression was pressed into two long horizontal mould boxes. The hollow centre was achieved by suspending a core of coarse rope

As can be seen in Professor John Smith's carefully posed photograph taken in the 1850s on the verandah of Drummoyne House, Sydney, imported cast iron furniture was popular with the wealthy classes. (*Sydney University Archives*)

twisted around an iron rod between the two boxes. The impression of the rope can usually be seen within the hollow base and capital of an old column.

About the same time that Horbury Terrace was being built in Macquarie Street (circa 1835) we can see from an advertisement in the *Sydney Herald* that baluster panels, gates and other cast iron items were being imported. In the late Victorian era, during Australia's mania for iron lace decoration, manufacturers occasionally had the impression of their foundry's name and the date of the pattern's registration for copyright cast onto

Australia's Iron Lace

A forest of slim-fluted iron columns with Ionic capitals support the *porte-cochère* and verandah of Retford Park at Bowral, New South Wales. This mansion was built for the wealthy retailer Anthony Horden in 1887 and the simple baluster pattern shows a restraint unusual in this flamboyant boom period. Retford Park is now owned by Mr James Fairfax.

Cast iron furniture was imported from England, mostly from Coalbrookdale. The beautifully cast bench features the nasturtium motif and, unlike locally made decorative iron, has a diamond shaped registration mark which indicates its year of manufacture as 1 March 1866. CBRALE Co. represents the Coalbrookdale Company which gave its name to this type of iron furniture.

Opposite This extraordinary *List of Goods* of the Hobart Town Foundery and Smithery of Robert Russell, dated 1835, takes back the documented date of locally manufactured ironwork to the 1830s. The list indicates the goods which he is 'enabled to manufacture' and may have been a little optimistic for the needs of the colony as he later moved to Sydney. However, given the number of elegant houses being built in Tasmania while his foundry was operating in Hobart it is likely that he supplied some of them with his 'Iron gates, railing, pallisades, balconies and invisible fences'. The note on the bottom is a warning to sticky fingered convicts against selling him any scrap metal they may have found before it was lost.

HOBART TOWN
FOUNDERY AND SMITHERY,
70,
ELIZABETH STREET.

Mr. *Dotson*

Sir,—Permit me to return my sincere thanks for the favours I have received from you. I beg to lay before you a list of Goods, which I am enabled to manufacture in this Colony, and no pains of mine will be spared to give satisfaction, both in quality and price, in the execution of your orders, which I take the liberty of soliciting.

I am, Sir,

Your obedient servant,

R. RUSSELL.

List of Goods:

Felling axes and mattocks made of the very best Swedish and common iron.

Wedges, mallets, rings, and hammers.

Kitchen ranges, with or without ovens, boilers, and salt kitts.

Smoke jacks, common and fine.

Water jacks, ditto ditto.

Wind-up jacks, single and double.

Ovens, square, cylindrical, and elliptic.

Hot tables, hot presses, and every article for cooking.

Common and cradle spits.

Jack screens and plate warmers, all iron, or wood lined with tin.

Beautiful brass fire dogs, new pattern.

Common ditto, in brass and iron.

Iron gates, railing, pallisades, balconies, and invisible fences.

House and shop carpenters' axes, adzes, hammers, and cramps.

All kinds of iron and steel work for carriages, particularly springs, done in the very best style.

Patent axles, with gun metal bushes, brass nave hoops, bell mouthed and brass caps for wheels.

All kinds of iron work for carts, drays, waggons, ploughs, harrows, barrows, and land rollers.

New iron ploughs of the most approved kinds.

Stone masons' hammers, picks, irons, &c., made and repaired.

Very superior scale beams, in brass and iron, with or without columns, and which I would recommend as the only safe system of weighing.

Draught engines and fountains, with pipes, tubes, &c., and also fitted up.

Shafts, spindles, brass bushes, and every article for mills.

Cranes for stores, quarries, &c., for lifting heavy articles.

Neat iron gates for paddocks.

Oven doors, kitchen fenders, and fire irons.

Malleable iron safes and chests for banks, merchants, &c. with proof locks.

Brand irons for casks, &c., cut in a very superior style.

A new pruning instrument from England, of real utility.

Brass and iron fire guards and fenders.

Trellises in iron and brass wire, to guard shop windows, &c. &c.

Brass and iron chandeliers for churches, halls, &c.

Taps, of all sizes, in gun metal and brass.

Copper and brass pumps, force and common lifting.

Bells and bell apparatus, for churches, ships, &c.

All kinds of iron work for ships.

Composition bolts, nails, dovetails, rudder bands, &c. for ditto.

Anchors, and chains of different sizes.

Whaling gear of all kinds, the harpoons will be particularly attended to.

Iron and brass work for saddlers, made and repaired on the shortest notice.

Very neat iron—cane-painted bedsteads.

Sofas, and swing cradles, very useful for the prevention of vermin.

Portable boilers, with furnaces, a very useful article for washing, as the water can be heated outside, and every inconvenience from heat and steam avoided.

Gass apparatus, for making and burning gass, made from coal, and oil, from drawings by eminent engineers.

Self-acting hinges for fly doors, so much used in the mother country for shops.

All kinds of rising and centre hinges, in brass and steel.

Register stoves, forest, cottage, and parlour grates.

T hinges, hooks and hinges, holdfasts, butts, bolts, picks, axes, mauls, wedges, and a great variety of articles ready for sale.

Steaming apparatus, very much used at home for preparing food for cattle and horses, a model of which may be seen at the foundery.

Gentlemen's houses, churches, &c. heated with warmed air or steam. The heating of dairies in this manner is now customary in Scotland, by which means Farmers are enabled to produce nearly as much butter, &c. in winter as in summer, where steaming apparatus is used.

Bells hung in the most substantial manner, every article almost being of my own manufacture, and intended to be strong, together with nearly 30 years experience in that line.

Copper boilers, with and without cocks.

Old brass work cleaned to look equal to new.

Bronzing, &c.

Printing presses and other articles for printers done in the best style.

Blowers for heating bakers' ovens, allowed to be the best method at home; a model may be seen at the foundery.

Steaming apparatus for tanning works, so much used at home for tanning leather.

☞ All kinds of old metals bought, but it is hoped none will make any offers, except of what is well come by.

Albion House in George Street, Launceston, Tasmania dates from about 1835.

the reverse side of the panel. Later in the century some British foundries, such as Macfarlane's Saracen Foundry in Glasgow, had their trademark on every casting, and in 1842 British manufacturers devised a code to register the date of manufacture, to be recorded on metal, wood, glass and ceramic objects using Roman numerals and letters. They are sometimes seen on imported cast iron hallstands or garden furniture but rarely on decorative ironwork. They are of more use to collectors of antique objects in the other materials rather than iron work and details are included in the *Antique Dealer and Collector's Guide*.

It is difficult in the absence of any identifying marks on decorative ironwork to say which of the early panels were imported and which were cast locally but it has been found that imported balcony panels were often double sided and locally cast ones either flat or hollowed on the reverse side.

The early 1840s are often cited as the approximate time for the earliest locally made decorative ironwork, but this has been corrected and the date brought forward to at least 1835 by a letter and advertisement of a *List of Goods* of the Hobart Town Foundery [*sic*] and Smithery of Robert Russell which is lodged in the Allport Library and Museum of Fine Arts in Hobart and was brought to my attention by the Librarian of Special Collections, Mr Geoffrey Stilwell.

Tasmania was settled in 1803 to ward off the unlikely event of French ambitions to establish a base there. In 1830 a financial depression in Scotland decided ironfounder Robert Russell and his wife and family of eleven

The wider panels on Albion House are the same as those on nearby Pleasant Banks at Evandale. The diagonals and central motif can be seen in Cottingham's *Director*.

children to migrate from Fife, Scotland to Hobart Town, Van Diemens Land. After they arrived in Hobart aboard the *Anne Jameson* in June 1832, Russell sold his 2000 acre grant and commenced a family engineering and foundry business with his three sons, Peter, Robert and John. In April 1835 Robert Russell used the back of a copy of his *List of Goods* to pen a sharp letter to John Dobson, solicitor, regarding a disputed account. The list of items manufactured in his foundry includes axes, ploughs and ovens so essential in an expanding colony as well as 'iron gates, railing, pallisades, balconies, and invisible fences' for the lovely Georgian homes and mansions then being built in Hobart and Launceston and on the farms of successful settlers.

Pleasant Banks at Evandale and Albion House in Launceston have identical single-sided baluster panels and a slightly different narrower one which appear in Cottingham's *Director*. Albion House is circa 1835 and Pleasant Banks was built in 1838 when Robert Russell and his sons were transferring their business to Sydney. Although Pleasant Banks was rebuilt after a fire in the 1870s its extensive ironwork is original. It would be nice to claim either or both their iron work as the work of Russell, but as neither carries any identifying mark this cannot be proved. However, more of the Russell family later.

Foundry names appear more frequently on locally made columns than on balusters and for mention of the first columns to be cast in New South Wales we must return to the often unreliable, but always entertaining, Joseph Fowles in *Sydney in 1848*:

> As one of the most prominent and interesting features of this locality, we must direct our attention to Mr Dawson's Foundry, which is generally considered to be the first in the Colony. As an instance of what can be done

Pencilled on the back of this old photograph is 'P. N. Russell's foundry works'. The foundry closed after much industrial unrest in 1873–74. His share in the family inheritance allowed the founder's nephew John Peter Russell, the Australian impressionist painter, to travel to Europe to follow his career with Rodin, Monet and Van Gogh. (*Mitchell Library*)

Above Pleasant Banks at Evandale is
surrounded by a balustrade of its original
ironwork. The panels, *right*, are similar to
those used on Hythe homestead (now
demolished). The Hythe panels are
documented in correspondence dated 1831
as being imported from England.

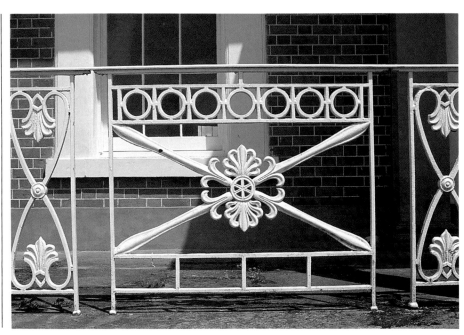

Early ironwork of unknown origin on Oakington (c. 1840) 15 Napoleon Street, Battery Point, Hobart.

in this Colony, it might be mentioned that iron work, of more than *four tons* weight, has been cast here with success. Mr Dawson has also, for multifarious reasons, an excellent high pressure steam engine, of eight horse power, which has been in constant use for the last eleven years. It was made on the premises, and, it is scarcely necessary to add, a finished piece of mechanism.[4]

Later in describing the interior of the Congregational Church in Pitt Street, Fowles explains:

The galleries ... are supported by fourteen cast iron columns of the Ionic order and fluted. These were cast by Mr Dawson, of Sydney, in a very neat and superior manner, and are the first series of ornamental columns cast in the Colony—they are finished in imitation bronze.[5]

The fourteen columns in the Congregational Church are not Ionic; neither, as we have seen, was Dawson's Australian Iron and Brass Foundry

JOHN S·PARKES ROYAL HOTEL.   IRONMONGERS.   FAMILY

HARPER & MOORE.   RUSSELL'S SYDNEY FOUNDRY   A. FA'R

John Sparke's fire prone Royal Hotel stands uneasily beside Peter Nicol Russell's Sydney Foundry in George Street. Peter Russell bought out James Blanch's foundry when he and his family arrived from Hobart Town where they had also run a foundry.

at 622 Lower George Street which he established in 1833, the first in the colony, although it seems to have been the most important. The steam engine mentioned by Fowles was one of the sights of Sydney and ran smoothly for over twenty years. Richard Dawson seems to have been very well liked and his resourcefulness and skills must have been appreciated in the expanding colony. He made cast iron wool presses for the squatters, and in 1853 when there was no graving dock in the port he cast a 'portable coffer dam' to allow access for repairs to the stern section of the General Screw Steam Shipping Company's SS *Croesus* which had limped into Sydney Harbour badly damaged.

In his advertisement in Ford's 1851 Sydney Directory Dawson's Australian Iron and Brass Foundry offered 'every description of Iron work' including 'Cast and Wrought Iron Railings and Balconies'. Unfortunately Dawson seems not to have cast his Australian Foundry trademark on his balcony panels or columns, as none have ever been sighted.

Mr James Blanch's foundry was on the south side of the Royal Hotel in George Street; in 1829 Mr A. White 'engineer and inventor' set up his rival business on the other side of the Royal. White invented a water filtering machine which could be inspected on his premises, warning that there was a spurious imitation in the neighbourhood, but trusting that 'a discerning public will admit that this is the highest praise which could be bestowed upon the inventor by those incapable of invention themselves, [when] they descend to become copyists'.

One wonders whether they ever settled their differences in the Royal Hotel which separated the two rivals and whose guests often complained about the smoke from their foundries. The manager, Mr J. Sparke must

AUSTRALIAN
IRON AND BRASS FOUNDRY,
ESTABLISHED 1833,
BY THE PRESENT PROPRIETOR.

MR. RICHARD DAWSON begs leave to inform his Friends and the Public, he still carries on the business of Founder and Shipsmith, where every description of Iron work may be had, of good material and best workmanship, on reasonable terms.

Hydraulic, Screw, and Rack Presses
Boiling-down Pots, *all sizes and not deficient in measure*
Patent Windlass
Ships' Cabooses
Cast Iron Pumps
Frills and Palls
Hawsepipes and Deck ditto
Crab Winches
Patent Stoves, for either wood, coal, or charcoal
Church and Ships' Bells
Down Spouting, Guttering, Hopper Heads, and Shoes
Cast and Wrought Iron Railing and Balconies
Wrought Iron Safes, (Fire-proof)
Ships' Pintals and Braces
Ships' Tanks
Mill Work, &c., &c.

Richard Dawson established his foundry in Sydney in 1833. His advertisement in Ford's *1851 Sydney Directory* lists 'Cast and Wrought Iron Railings and Balconies' but unfortunately he did not put his trademark on his ornamental castings. Mr Dawson's fourteen columns can still be seen in the Congregational Church in Pitt Street.

have been fed up with both, especially on St Patrick's Day in 1840, when, according to Fowles,

> a drunken carter, who had been indulging in copious libations to St Patrick, amused himself by smoking his pipe in an adjoining stable, belonging to Mr Blanch; and the straw igniting, the immense stack of buildings was speedily in flames.[6]

The fire was contained and a major disaster averted by speedily levelling some of the nearby wooden buildings but the total damage was estimated at £20 000.

The optimistic Mr Sparke rebuilt the new five-storey Royal Hotel with a predominantly wooden frontage, and in 1842 Blanch's foundry was

Above and *above right* Bubb and Rees Victoria Foundry columns at Windsor, New South Wales.

Below right Bubb and Rees grille columns were added to this row of circa 1837 terrace houses at Windsor, known as the Doctor's House, at a later date.

purchased by Mr Peter Nichol Russell, the second son of Robert Russell, who had left Hobart in 1838 for the better opportunities Sydney had to offer. Peter and his brothers operated a foundry, Russell Bros in Queens Square, for several years before he opted out to buy James Blanch's foundry for £2000 to be paid off over three years. Russell renamed it the Sydney Foundry and Engineering Works, paid off the purchase price within two years and received large contracts from the New South Wales government including the ironwork for Victoria Barracks and Darlinghurst jail. He later manufactured gunboats for the New Zealand government for use during the Maori Wars.

Unlike Dawson, Russell had his company's name *P. N. Russell & Co.* cast on the base of his fluted columns which can still be seen on some old Sydney mansions, including Rosemont at Edgecliff. Russell's Sydney Foundry closed in the mid 1870s after much industrial trouble and after selling up his property in Australia he returned to England. In 1895 he

1850s buildings in Sydney's Rocks area often have columns bearing the Bubb and Rees Victoria Foundry trademark. Sydney's most famous iron landmark can be seen in the distance.

made a gift of £50 000 to Sydney University to found a school of engineering—on the condition that it would be named after him. One of his early cast columns stands as a memorial to him outside the Peter Nicol Russell Building at Sydney University.

The 1855 Sydney Directory lists Bubb and Temperley Victoria Foundry as being located at 10 Victoria Street Sydney. Later changing to Bubb and Son and then Bubb and Rees, their Victoria Foundry trademark was cast onto their open work columns which can be seen on many 1850s and 1860s vintage houses in Sydney and nearby towns such as Windsor. None of their trade catalogues have survived and little is known about the Victoria Foundry but as their castings are still so common it can be assumed that they specialised in domestic iron decoration, and speculate

This towered homestead at Orange, New South Wales either used imported ironwork or had it specially cast locally as it has not been seen elsewhere in Australia. (*New South Wales Government Printer*)

that it was in the late 1850s that locally made castings took over largely from imported.

It was at this time that iron frills were becoming so popular that they were being added not only to new buildings but to older ones as well. In the early 1860s cast open work columns from the Victoria Foundry were added to the verandah of Elizabeth Farm at Parramatta, built by John Macarthur in 1793–94—the oldest building in Australia. A group of three terraces overlooking the Hawkesbury River at Windsor, New South Wales are known as the Doctor's House. When they were built around 1837, the balcony was probably unroofed; the open columns from the Victoria Foundry were added in the early 1860s.

The late 1850s and the 1860s saw the proliferation of double-storey terrace houses that are still a distinctive feature of Australian cities. Like the iron lace which was lavished on them, the Australian attitude to terrace

These sandstone and brick terraces in York Street, Sydney were photographed in 1871 but the wear on their steps indicates that they had been standing for some time. The vertical designs on the balustrades and the open grille columns show a restraint which was to disappear during the forthcoming boom period. (*New South Wales Government Printer*)

houses must seem quirky to an impartial observer. They were at first immensely popular; when they fell from grace they quickly deteriorated into slums and as most were approaching their hundredth birthday during the 1960s and 1970s, they once again became fashionable. One generation of Australians was eager to get out of its terraces, the next was paying extraordinarily high prices to get back into them and whereas the previous owners had torn down the iron lace to sell as scrap, the next were frantically putting it back up, often upside down, or replacing it with aluminium replicas in out-of-character wooden frames.

Areas such as Sydney's Paddington, and Parkville and Carlton in Melbourne, are the most spectacularly successful unplanned restoration projects ever seen and the terrace houses packed into these areas have produced some of the steepest increases in real estate values in the world.

Despite the rash of glossy coffee table books on Australian

Nineteenth century terrace houses are still a feature of Australian cities.

Left Wrought and cast iron panels on terraces in Carrington Street, Adelaide, and unusual split-level terraces in Ballarat, Victoria.

Below 'Concertina terraces' in Sydney's Paddington.

architecture dealing with homesteads, colonial mansions or shearing sheds, very little has been published on Australia's terrace houses which lack a definitive architectural history. Perhaps they are still a little too humble in the minds of some Australians, or there is still a large segment of the population for whom these revived terrace house suburbs still conjure up memories of a harsh depression childhood spent in them. Real estate values are certainly very high in Sydney's Surry Hills, but Ruth Park's compassionate slum classic *Harp in the South*, about the lives of the Irish-Australian Darcy family who lived in a ramshackle terrace house 12A Plymouth Street (renumbered by the landlord as 13 was considered unlucky by the Irish), was set there in the late 1940s—well within recent memory. The gentrification of similar areas in Sydney and Melbourne has been rapid

Balconies, ironwork and raised party walls remained distinctive features of Sydney terraces until the end of the century.

and spectacular. As most of Australia's surviving iron lace is worn by terrace houses and pubs, rather than Greenway's magnificent churches or the perfectly symmetrical Georgian colonial homesteads, terrace houses and pubs are the main focus of this book.

On the edge of this vast and virtually unexplored continent, terrace houses were built during the 1830s in the style of drizzle-bound London, complete with a parapet which among other uses, helped to prevent piled up snow from falling onto passers-by. It is easy to mock the lack of imagination of Australia's earliest builders, but when Phillip's unskilled convicts were struggling with the unfamiliar gnarled timbers and the bewildering climatic conditions, as well as trying to lay their locally made bricks while faced with a critical shortage of local lime deposits, they were wise to stay with the methods and styles that they knew. The experience was not unique to Australia; India, for example, had absurd Victorian Gothic cottages at hill stations such as Simla and Darjeeling in the Himalayas, and English country houses were built on Corfu and in the West Indies. When a bizarre band of Australian utopians sailed for Paraguay in the 1890s, they built Queensland homesteads complete with verandahs on their socialist colony 'Nueva Australia' in the Paraguayan *chaco*. When some later moved south to the cold and windy Patagonian desert in Argentina to take up land to start sheep *estancias*, they built their shearing sheds in imitation

Lyon's Terrace from Joseph Fowles' *Sydney in 1848*. The origins of terrace houses in England are obscure but little distinction was made during the early 1800s between country and city housing and terraces were built in tiny villages as well as in suburbs of industrial towns spawned by the Industrial Revolution in its early stages when distinctions between town and country overlapped. This may help us understand why in the 1830s and 1840s, on the edge of a huge unmapped continent, English colonists and speculators built their terraces in Hobart, Sydney and Windsor.

of those they had worked in on the hot dusty plains of western Queensland.

From tradition comes innovation, and from innovation, style. The crowded and compact terraces, with their origins in Bath or Bristol, added their verandahs in deference to the antipodean sun, and so adapted to inner-city living in Australia.

Samuel Lyons had a turbulent career as a convict before becoming one of Sydney's leading business men and builder of terraces. A London Jewish tailor, he arrived in Sydney on board the convict transport *Marquis of Wellington* in January 1815 under a long sentence of transportation for theft. He absconded, was recaptured and flogged, only to escape again with the same result. In 1819 he was once again tied to the triangles and received 200 lashes, enough to kill some men, for stealing government stores, and was sentenced to four years at Newcastle—a particularly brutal penal settlement for the most incorrigible convicts.

In 1822 he married a young Irish woman Mary Murphy and seems to have started life anew. He opened a shop in Sydney and when he received his absolute pardon in 1832 he was one of Sydney's leading auctioneers. He made a brief visit to England and on his return to Sydney, he built a row of terrace houses in what is now Liverpool Street opposite Hyde Park. Lyons is said to have spent £5000 on each of the five three-storey houses in the row and on their completion had his name and the date set in an entablature on the parapet S. LYONS 1841.

Lyons Terrace was a departure from the Georgian streetscape of Sydney shown in Fowles' *Sydney in 1848* (remembering that Fowles showed only the dress circle and not the slums and hovels around the Rocks and Brickfields Hill), and it also set the architectural character of most of the terraces that were to be built in Australian cities and towns during that century. To conform with new building regulations the party walls extended one foot six inches above the roofline. Unlike previously built terraces it was set back from the street, which provided space for a small front garden behind an iron railing fence. The balconies had balustrades of

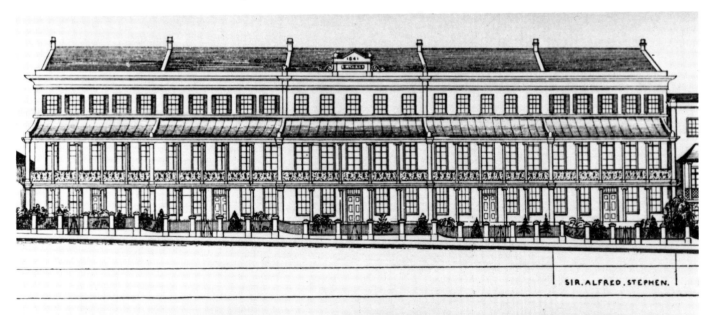

SIR. ALFRED. STEPHEN.

LYON'S TERRACE   HYDE PARK.

Lyons Terrace, the third block of houses on the left, was still standing at the turn of the century.

decorative ironwork which were to become the most distinctive feature of Australian terrace houses. Lyons Terrace was a posh address; it bespeaks the bizarre origins of Australia's white history, where the main industries for a long time were the commission of crime and its punishment, that the tenants of the ex-convict landlord included the Chief Justice of New South Wales, a judge of the Supreme Court and a leading barrister. As a further touch of class, a Miss Moore conducted a school for young ladies at number 1 Lyons Terrace. The five houses were demolished in 1905 and old photographs suggest that the ironwork on the balconies was similar to an early pattern that can still be seen in Tasmania.

In England the Regency period after the Napoleonic wars coincided with stringent financial times. Houses became smaller, surfaces plainer and decoration more discrete. These early cast iron patterns, seen only in Sydney and Tasmania, date from this period. As the wealth of England improved, there was a demand for comparatively wealthy middle class housing and by the 1840s there was an enthusiastic use of cast iron decoration. But once the middle class took it up it ceased being popular with the English upper class, who gave up using it prolifically. Most of the extensive use of iron decoration on high quality houses in England dates from the early period.

Cast iron decoration was often added to older buildings at a later date. The gracious homestead on Ivanhoe station, at Keyneton, South Australia, *above*, and Wybalena at Hunters Hill, Sydney, *right*, both had their standard iron lacework added in later Victorian times.

Examination with a magnifying glass on a clearer copy of Holtermann's 1874 mansion at North Sydney shows it to display the same pattern as the balcony of the Australian Joint Stock Bank *below*, at 373 George Street during the same period. The pattern is a French one from the mid nineteenth century Parisian catalogue of *Barbezat et Cie*, whose panels were perhaps imported and then duplicated. (*New South Wales Government Printer*)

Right The wider bird panel and the matching narrow balusters are often seen separately or together. They are among the most frequently seen patterns in Sydney and still appeared in the "Sun" foundry catalogue as late as 1914.

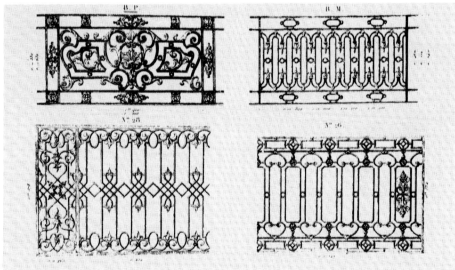

The use of cast iron decoration in Australia did not have this class consciousness. After the gold rushes skilled labour was scarce in Australia and the high cost of that labour, when available, made cast iron more attractive to the moneyed classes, especially as they were newly moneyed. But its use was not exclusive to the rich. We can see from advertisements (see pages 36 and 45) that cast iron panels were being produced locally in the 1850s (and probably much earlier) and old photographs of later inner city working-class terraces show that they were being used enthusiastically on these as well. There seemed to be no marked difference in ornamental taste between men of wealth and power and the working class; when Bernard Otto Holtermann used part of the fortune he made from gold to build his towered mansion at North Sydney in 1874, it wore a French iron lace pattern which was common on country hotels and the future slum terraces in Surry Hills and Redfern.

Right Pattern 28 from the Parisian *Barbezat et Cie* catalogue was photographed in Paul Gauguin's favourite village of Pont Aven in Brittany, France; in William Street, Paddington, *above*; in Sydney's Rocks area, *below left*; and in Rush Street Woollahra, *below right*. (See also page 119 at Hill End.)

Above Another French pattern was photographed in Rue du Téhéran in Paris' fashionable 8me arrondissement and is frequently seen in Sydney's Surry Hills *right*.

Elegant homesteads, complete with towers and private ballrooms, were built by successful squatters on their sheep runs. Some used imported ironwork but most dressed their balconies and verandahs with the same ironwork patterns as were on the shops and pubs in the nearby country towns.

There are few middle-of-the-century terraces left in Sydney. Most were too close to the centre of the city to have survived the street widening programmes and many were demolished around the turn of the century for commercial and retail developments. Old photographs, taken just prior to their demolition, give us an idea of the appearance and the iron ornament used on these forerunners of the more lavishly decorated terraces which were to ensue during the building boom of the following decades.

The only iron work on the 1850s Regency style Rose Terrace in William Street, (Rose Terrace is painted beneath the fourth and fifth first-storey windows) are the cast iron balconettes, with a pattern with more void than fill, and similar to earlier imported patterns on Horbury Terrace.

The only ironwork on Rose Terrace is the cast iron balconettes.

These late 1850s or early 1860s sandstone terraces in William Street, Sydney, were photographed prior to their demolition in 1916. The iron lace pattern on the balconies has almost disappeared from Sydney and the pattern on the verandah below the French Cleaners' sign has vanished altogether.

The terraces above were also built in William Street during the late 1850s or early 1860s but balconies and verandahs have been added as protection from the sun. Flat grille columns on the balconies were dispensed with by later Victorian terrace designers; in this case they seem to have been laid horizontally on the balconies and used as a fringe as well. The balustrade pattern is fuller and shows a departure from the sparse earlier designs to more florid ornamentation. These double-sided panels are now rare in Sydney but can still be seen on contemporary houses at 357 Glebe Point Road, Glebe and in Darley Street, Kings Cross.

Cast iron then, in the 1850s, was the height of fashion, enjoying a popularity that was to become almost obsessional three decades later.

2

Popularity

The ornamental and durable castings ... that have grown in favour so rapidly during the past few years ...

Queenslander *20 May 1882*

'Australian architecture', wrote Professor J. M. Freeland in his *Architecture in Australia* (1968), 'left its innocence behind when gold was discovered in May 1851.' Melbourne, then, lost such innocence at the tender age of sixteen. Two rival groups of settlers, under a cloud of official disapproval, crossed Bass Strait from Tasmania in the mid 1830s and settled on the banks of the Yarra River which was considered to be 'a good place for a village'. Governor Bourke from New South Wales visited the settlement and in March 1837 gave the enterprising settlers his official sanction, christening the township Melbourne, after Britain's Prime Minister.

Melbourne, the capital of Victoria, is probably the world's most enthusiastic Victorian city. The city grew up and matured during Queen Victoria's reign and indulged in the many disputing and ostentatious architectural styles of that period. Rich at the age of sixteen after the discovery of gold, Melbourne's 'desperate sophisticates' as Robin Boyd called them, imported the Gothic, Italianate and Classical fashions of the 'war of the styles' which was raging in Europe; 'the churches were mainly Gothic, the public buildings leant to Rome'.[7] Entire streets in Melbourne, as well as former gold centres such as Ballarat, remain much the same as when they were built during the boom period which reached its peak in the late 1880s. In some commercial areas there is now a split level fashion, with modern shop fronts at street level and, above, the lavishly embellished and stuccoed upper level.

Melbourne has been called an architectural frolic, a Victorian museum and time capsule—and a practical joke. If unprepared for it, Melbourne's Victoriana can give a visitor a slightly amused surprise, rather like seeing the statue of Queen Victoria or the Gothic Revival railway station in Bombay. But Melbourne's architects and planners were entirely serious

and earnest about their creation—they wanted their city to display all the finery of current architectural fashion as an expression of their confidence and pride in the colony 'Victoria the Golden'. An enlightened parliament was elected and in 1853 almost 200 new buildings were going up each month. When independence as a separate colony was proclaimed in 1851 Victoria had a population of 76 000; ten years later it had risen to half a million.

'.. who shall define the limits of (Melbourne's) future dignity and splendour?' asked the *Australian Home Guardian* in November 1856. 'The prophetic eye beholds its wide and spacious thoroughfares fringed with edifices worthy of the wealth of its citizens and corresponding in architectural pretensions with the greatness of the commercial transactions of their occupants.'

The lavish Melbourne style of ironwork uses matching elements, round columns, and bulky wooden handrails.

Unlike those of Sydney, her northern rival, Melbourne's streets were indeed spacious and leafy and followed a plan the Sydney office 'generally approved as suitable for laying out a new township'. This was implemented by the Assistant Surveyor-General of New South Wales, Robert Hoddle. To help defray the expenses of the new colony the government auctioned off land along the Yarra River which showed huge speculative gains as the colony expanded. Hoddle bought two city blocks for himself for £54; they were worth £250 000 when he died in 1881.

Melbourne, unlike the older colonies of New South Wales and Tasmania, did not have a Georgian colonial period that had its roots in the eighteenth century and branches which continued into the nineteenth century. Melbourne's builders indulged in the confusion of styles which abounded in Europe after the mid-1800s: Gothic, Italianate, French,

Como, beautifully restored by the National Trust (Victoria). Its ironwork was imported from Scotland.

St Stephens, a prefabricated iron church which stood in Macquarie Street, Sydney, photographed in 1871. (*New South Wales Government Printer*)

Moorish and 'picturesque chateau'. The Georgian-influenced colonial style of the two older colonies was firmly rejected as the ugly reminder of the stern military architecture of a penal colony—entirely unsuited to the self-important and gold rich colony of Victoria.

Dr E. G. Robertson, whose research and books led to the revival of interest in Australia's iron lace and Victorian architecture, maintained that his native Melbourne displayed more iron lace decoration than any other city in the world.

It was, however, cast iron's more practical and utilitarian cousin, galvanised iron, which first helped solve Melbourne's critical need for housing. Huge quantities of corrugated sheets were imported from Britain and used to clad the walls and leaky roofs of the makeshift houses; they were often placed over the wooden shingles which were retained as insulation.

Cast iron panels and fence railings were imported and used on early mansions such as Como, which still stands, beautifully restored, on the south bank of the Yarra. On 12 June 1856, Scott, Clow and Prebble's Richmond Foundry (Melbourne's first) ran an advertisement in the *Australian Builder and Practical Mechanic* offering to supply 'ornamental railings' as well as heavy quartz crushing batteries for the goldfields. Others quickly followed to meet Melbourne's insatiable building demands—by 1888 one foundry in Geelong, Humble and Nicholson, had a works covering over three acres and employing 120 men. In a burgeoning colony such as Victoria foundries produced not only decorative domestic ironwork but cast iron stoves, wool presses and agricultural machinery.

A Victorian public servant placed an order with a Scottish foundry for the prefabrication and shipment of an iron house to live in during his retirement, but died six months before its arrival at Cunningham's Pier, Geelong, late in 1855. The assortment of cast iron arches and columns, corrugated roofing iron and stacks of 12 mm thick sheets lay unclaimed on the wharf until the port authorities decided to auction it. It was purchased for a small sum by Geelong businessman Mr Alfred Douglas, who had the heavy iron jig-saw puzzle carted to higher ground. On a site overlooking

STEPHEN'S CHURCH SYDNEY

A complete restoration of Corio Villa is in progress and a few sheets of the heavy guage corrugated iron from the roof and some of the cast iron guttering are being replaced after 130 years of service.

The columns of Corio Villa conceal drainage pipes from the roof.

Corio Bay, with a distant view of the You Yangs, Corio Villa, a unique Australian building, was sorted out and assembled on bluestone foundations.

When the present owner, Mr Murray McAllister, purchased Corio Villa in 1961 it was in a dilapidated condition and had narrowly escaped being demolished. Some cast iron roof guttering had corroded and Mr McAllister has had replicas cast at a Melbourne foundry. Some parts of the roof and the rear walls have also required replacing; this presented a more difficult problem as the Scottish galvanised iron sheets are 3 mm thick and have wide corrugations of a type rarely seen in Australia. However, the owner has been able to salvage sufficient over the years from old homesteads and factories throughout Victoria.

Another prefabricated iron house still standing and in excellent condition 130 years after its assembly is Wingecarribbee at Bowral, New

Wingecarribbee, at Bowral, New South Wales. The entire house—fireplaces, floorboards, doors and ceilings as well as the cast iron parapet and heavy gauge corrugated iron roofing and walls—was imported from England. The house is extraordinarily sound and the ironwork has no sign of corrosion or rust.

South Wales. John Oxley, son of the explorer, ordered the house from a British manufacturer in 1853 when all of the local building tradesmen had left for the goldfields but he was not able to get it erected until 1857 when conditions were returning to normal. Wingecarribbee is still occupied by Oxley's descendants.

Some 'iron pot' churches were also imported to Melbourne and Sydney but they proved to be infernally hot and difficult to insulate. Some iron houses were also built in Sydney, according to Professor J. M. Freeland in his *Architecture in Australia*:

> A large prefabricated house in Woolloomooloo became the headquarters of, and gave its name to, one of the most feared pushes to roam the jungles around Woolloomooloo and Paddington—The Iron House Mob.[8]

Conrad Martins sketched an early cast iron house at Kirribilli called The Dingle, thought to have been near Waruda Avenue; this has also disappeared.

Cast iron houses were not a success in Australia, unlike the United States, especially New York which still has some enormous cast iron fronted buildings. Cast iron remained immensely popular as showy eye-catching decoration and was used structurally in columns, but it was cast iron's Cinderella sister, corrugated galvanised iron, which spread out across the entire continent as a building material. It was light and easily transported and it had the added bonus of being able to collect rainwater from the roof—it is hard to imagine an Australian country town or homestead without it.

Melbourne's extravagant Victoriana in iron and stucco.

Gold, and the waves of people who came seeking it, made Melbourne the centre of Australian growth and the fashion leader in architectural trends. Those who found gold stayed and built their mansions; the unlucky ones also stayed to share the prosperity it left in its wake. Tradesmen found an avid labour market and higher wages than they were used to receiving in Europe and elsewhere.

The full impact of what we call the Victorian era commenced in the 1860s and set the tone and style for the following three decades. It embodied an unquestionable faith and confidence in Empire and material progress—'evidence of progression' was the contemporary term—which took the utmost pride in displaying its wealth. The strict formality and the narrow morals of behaviour did not restrain the Victorians' need for showy display. Appearances were all important—within the house and without—and the rectitude and morals were often as superficial as the showy facades of the houses.

Suburbs of exotic Victoriana burgeoned as the larger parcels of land were sub-divided, usually with the sole view of maximising profits, though the streets of Melbourne, unlike those of Sydney, remained wide. Those who leant to the Gothic hung wooden barge boards from the gables of their high pitched roofs, but during the 1870s the 'classic' gained ascendancy and the terraces of the working class and the free standing houses of the wealthier carried the full and extravagant paraphernalia of iron and stucco classically inspired decoration. Parapets were moulded with motifs of garlands, swags and masks and surmounted with shells and urns, their designs are easily recognised in Victorian pattern books of Greek and Roman ornament of antiquity. Brick and stone walls were stuccoed and lined to imitate dressed stone and dividing fire walls were impressed with classical face masks, staring blandly across the street. The patterns of cast iron decoration became more blatantly eye-catching and extravagant and took their final departure from the thin ribbon-like tendrils and swirls it had inherited from wrought iron design. Melbourne foundries were able to register the copyright of their designs for their own exclusive use, the first being recorded on 8 April 1870.

Iron lace with matching elements throughout drips like wysteria from these two classic Melbourne facades at 52 and 54 Powlett Street, East Melbourne.

The separate elements in some of these patterns were sometimes animated by picking them out in different colours, a fact that is often overlooked or forgotten in modern restoration. The colours used were not always bright; stripping back a panel to its original colour often reveals a muddy green or brown, used separately or, occasionally, together.

Some of the future slum terraces of Carlton and Fitzroy were thrown up with little heed to sanitation, light and ventilation but all faced the street smothered in a display of superficial trimmings suggesting wealth rendered in iron and plaster. The rich built their mansions with equally conspicuous and useless towers, round and tall or in a squared and block-like Italianate fortress style. The choice of iron patterns made from the foundry catalogues was arbitrary and impersonal, the same patterns can be seen on Toorak mansions and Carlton terraces.

However there were some spectacular exceptions, such as the specially cast 'opera box' balconies on 74 and 76 Park Street, South Yarra, two of

74 and 76 Park Street, South Yarra, two of the loveliest iron lace houses in Australia.

the loveliest iron lace houses in Australia. Illawarra House, a National Trust property at Toorak, was built by the Melbourne land speculator Charles James in 1890–91 and has a wild exuberance of lace designed to match the flamboyance of its style. There is unique domestic iron lace on another National Trust property, Barwon Park, a 42-room bluestone mansion at Inverleigh Road, Winchelsea, Victoria. Built in 1869 to the design of Davidson and Henderson of Geelong and Melbourne, the elaborate cast iron was specially designed for the house. In the centre of the single-storey verandah a double-storey portico carries the crest, motto and initials of the owner together with the date of building. The decorative elements of the cast iron design were also used within the house, on the staircase balustrade and on the plaster cornice of the drawing room.

Above right Thomas Austin chartered a ship to import the cedar, oak, marble and glass used in his 42 room mansion at Barwon Park near Winchelsea. The elaborate ironwork was designed for the house. The pattern on each side of the portico includes the crest, motto and initials of the owners as well as the date 1869. The same pattern seen on the balcony railing *above* is used within the house on the balustrade of the magnificent oak staircase. The pattern also features on the plaster cornices of several rooms. Thomas Austin liked to play the role of sporty English squire and is better remembered for his unfortunate decision to import ten pairs of wild European rabbits for release at Barwon Park as sport for the shooting parties he loved to host. These rabbits now have unnumbered millions of destructive descendants throughout pastoral Australia.

An extravagant boom style 'wedding cake' house in Nicholson Street, Melbourne, awaits restoration.

Robin Boyd had only lukewarm enthusiasm for the iron lace in his native Melbourne, calling it 'the pie filling in the rows of two-storey terrace houses'. Writing in 1960, trying to explain its lavish and ostentatious use in Melbourne's domestic architecture and the blatant desire to make wealth or success conspicuous for all to see, he quotes the Van Diemen's Land *Monthly Magazine*, which in 1835, years before the great gold discoveries and the sudden wealth which followed, also commented on this dominant characteristic of the newly rich and the

> ... incongruities in buildings, furniture, dress and equipage which we fear cannot fail to strike the observant stranger. This love of display, so inconsistent with the character and situation of settlers in a new country, may indeed have partly originated in each wishing to impress upon his neighbour a due sense of his previous circumstances, and standing in society. But, whatever the cause, the effect is too apparent.[9]

Opposite Ellimatta in Drummond Street, Carlton, has all the characteristics of Melbourne's decorative ironwork: deep arching brackets which match motifs on the balustrade and round columns. The gate post is cast iron and even the heads of the iron palisade fence are elaborate.

29 Sackville Street, Kew displays a deep apron of ironwork, beautifully cast and maintained. The human face in the verandah frieze *below* has a porcelain-like finish.

Some unusual unregistered Melbourne designs.

A thin swirling pattern designed to imitate wrought iron complete with metal collars binding the tendrils together.

A rare floral pattern incorporating ears of wheat.

Perhaps the origins can be found in the miseries of the earlier convict days when the newly emancipated or financially successful wished to declare their new status. In Melbourne, newly and more opulently rich, with the head-spinning excitement of land speculation during its building boom, the ostentatious impulse was stronger than elsewhere. The excesses of ornamentation, just when it appeared to have gone as far as possible, always managed to assert themselves. Melbourne's cast iron designs reached a higher degree of elaboration during its 'boom period' than did those in any other part of Australia, or even, perhaps, the world.

Social conditions were changing rapidly as were opportunities to attain wealth in land speculation. That keen observer of Australian urban life, R. E. N. Twopeny, noted in 1883, 'This land speculation is quite a feature of Australian life, and at certain periods it is difficult to lose money by it'.[10] The hysteria of Melbourne's land boom raised eyebrows even in Sydney which had seen the family fortunes of its 'bunyip aristocracy' made from land grabbing and rum dealing in an earlier age. *The Bulletin*, never at a loss for invective or the opportunity to deliver a broadside across

This lion's head pattern appears on terrace houses in Canning Street, North Melbourne and has not been sighted elsewhere.

A horse and jockey pattern at 458 William Street, Melbourne can also be seen in Mitchell Street, Glebe, Sydney.

the Murray, in November 1893 offered the advice that 'the policy of the continent at large should be to declare Victoria an infected province until its moral character has been renovated and its reputation restored'.[11]

The boom period, which fed and depended upon ever increasing speculation, finally burst, amid sensational scandals of fraudulent practices by leading figures in business and politics. During the harsh economic depression which followed, building in Melbourne stopped dead at the point where its florid Victorian architecture was at the full swing of its pendulum. When building resumed the natural reaction to a style which had reached satiety was to swing away in the opposite direction. Both Federation Melbourne and Sydney were suddenly ashamed of their cast iron and terraces.

When the worst of the harrowing depression had passed building slowly recommenced in the stolid Federation style and it is difficult to believe that only a few years, and not eons, separate it from the wild extravagance of the Boom Period.

Top The iron fence on 219 Stanley Street, North Adelaide appears in the 1887 edition of the *Illustrated Catalogue of Fulton's Castings* (page 175).

Above Iron fence in Gawler, South Australia.

Adelaide was spared the excesses of a Rum Corps and land boom speculators and enjoyed the farsighted planning of its Surveyor General, Colonel William Light. His legacy of orderliness is still apparent in its park-like atmosphere and the polite manners of its inhabitants. Adelaide's cast iron seems to have been influenced more by imported geometric English patterns; when panels were produced locally they remained more conservative than in Sydney and Melbourne.

The bluestone terraces and houses of North Adelaide wear their ironwork more discreetly and without the excessive opulence of the eastern cities. Adelaide's ironwork is used with a lighter touch and features most noticeably as brackets and fringes on single-storey verandahs and in gates and fence panels mounted on low brick walls, in contrast to Sydney and Melbourne where iron palisade fences are more common. As in Victoria, open grille columns that are common in Sydney are rare in South Australia.

Despite the richness of its cast iron decoration relatively few registrations were made for copyright, and most of these were for ventilator grilles and grave railings. However, the provenance of Adelaide's cast iron can be found in two lavishly illustrated foundry catalogues held in the South Australian Collection of the Library of South Australia: *Illustrated Catalogue of Fulton's Castings 2nd edn, 1887* and *C. Stewart and A. C. Harley's "Sun" Foundry illustrated catalogue 1st edn, 1897*. The library also holds a second edition of the *"Sun" Foundry catalogue* dated 1914.

The Fulton catalogue contains many patterns from the 1882 edition of

Above and middle Weeroni, 151 East Terrace, Adelaide has a delicately cast panel which appears in the Fulton catalogue (page 175) as well as the earlier Saracen Foundry Catalogue (page 174).

Below Many of North Adelaide's gates and fences can also be seen in the 1897 edition of C. Stewart and A.C. Harley's "Sun" Foundry Catalogue (page 176).

The only information we have on some foundries is from their advertisements, such as this for the Vulcan Iron Works from an 1885 directory. Most foundry catalogues have disappeared.

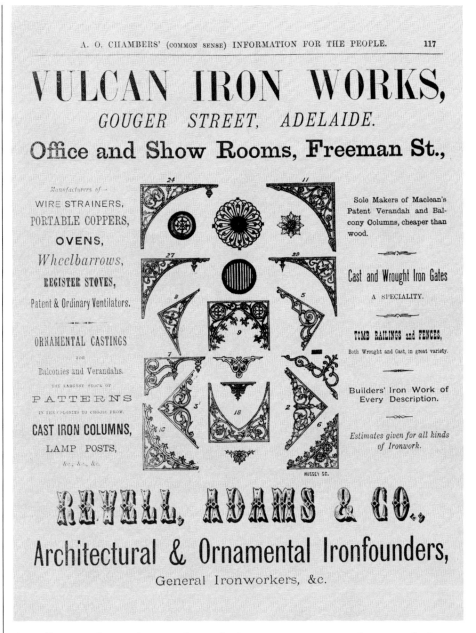

VULCAN IRON WORKS,

GOUGER STREET, ADELAIDE.

Office and Show Rooms, Freeman St.,

Manufacturers of —
WIRE STRAINERS,
PORTABLE COPPERS,
OVENS,
Wheelbarrows,
REGISTER STOVES,
Patent & Ordinary Ventilators.

ORNAMENTAL CASTINGS
FOR
Balconies and Verandahs.
THE LARGEST STOCK OF
PATTERNS
IN THE COLONIES TO CHOOSE FROM.
CAST IRON COLUMNS,
LAMP POSTS,
&c., &c., &c.

Sole Makers of Maclean's Patent Verandah and Balcony Columns, cheaper than wood.

Cast and Wrought Iron Gates
A SPECIALITY.

TOMB RAILINGS and FENCES,
Both Wrought and Cast, in great variety.

Builders' Iron Work of Every Description.

Estimates given for all kinds of Ironwork.

REVELL, ADAMS & CO.,

Architectural & Ornamental Ironfounders,

General Ironworkers, &c.

the *Illustrated Catalogue of Macfarlane's Castings*. Walter Macfarlane's Saracen foundry was the world's largest in its day, covering ten acres with its own railway and satellite suburb of Possilpark on the outskirts of Glasgow, Scotland. The Saracen foundry exported its castings throughout the world, from Bangkok to Buenos Aires, and, apparently Adelaide. Many of the castings illustrated in both catalogues also show almost identical measurements, those in the Fulton catalogue often being fractionally smaller which suggests that Macfarlane's panels may have been used as master patterns in moulding. The resulting panels would then contract to the slightly smaller dimensions.

The "Sun" Foundry catalogue is larger than the Fulton and includes some of the more extravagant patterns registered in Melbourne as well as an outstanding array of general cast iron items such as folding theatre seats, garden fountains, baker's ovens, road rollers and sanitary ware. The "Sun" catalogue also features some of the Macfarlane & Co., Saracen Foundry, Glasgow designs which appeared in the earlier Fulton catalogue. Both display a large range of brackets, fringes and the distinctive iron gates and fences which distinguish Adelaide's streets from the eastern cities.

South Australian towns and homesteads also have an understated and graceful touch of cast iron.

Gawler, like Adelaide, was surveyed and planned by Colonel Light. James Martins established his Phoenix Foundry there in the early 1850s and later produced some of the panels to decorate the houses and hotels which make Gawler one of the prettiest iron lace towns in Australia.

Martindale, a bluestone house in Duffield Street, built in 1872, was the residence of James Martins' nephew and foundry manager, John Felix Martins; the foundry by this time had grown into an enormous enterprise. Martindale is now a convalescent home. The beautiful verandah panels were cast from an Adelaide pattern by Thompson's Foundry in Gawler

This iron monument in Gawler tells its own story.

This copy of the 6th edition, 1882 of *Macfarlane's Castings* bears the stamp of the Scottish company's Sydney agent, Neave & Co., and is reproduced with the kind permission of its owner, Mr Neil Champion of Paddington, Sydney. Copies made from Macfarlane's Saracen Foundry castings can still be seen from Adelaide to Townsville, Queensland.

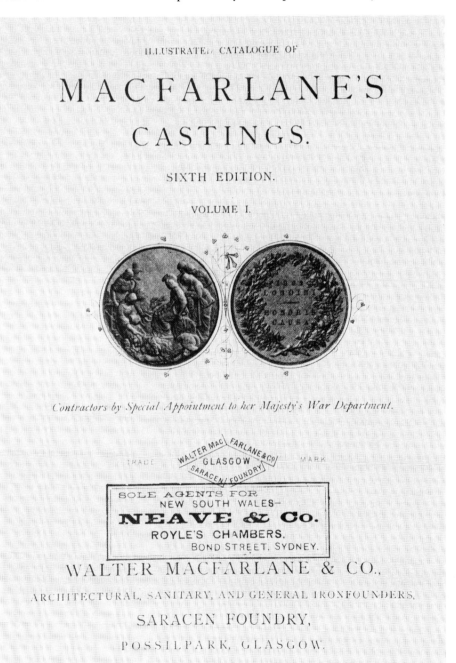

Lovely Martindale, Gawler. Its balcony's ironwork was cast locally by Thompson's Foundry using an Adelaide pattern.

and added in 1895; the pattern appears in Adelaide's "Sun" Foundry catalogue on page 177. The huge cast iron urns at the foot of the steps are thought to have been cast by Martin's Phoenix Foundry.

Kapunda, to the north of the Barossa Valley, is an old copper mining town which 'boomed' in the 1840s. Like other towns of its size it had a foundry, Hawke & Co., founded in 1857 and still trading as an engineering firm under the same name. This foundry supplied Kapunda with its decorative ironwork as well as heavy mining and agricultural equipment. Mr R. Anderson is manager of the Hawke & Co. workshop and has been employed at the foundry for 49 years. He told me:

> Iron lace panels were only ever a sideline at a country foundry like ours—agricultural equipment kept us going. We used Adelaide and Melbourne panels to make our moulds. I remember just after World War Two when we couldn't get pig iron, the boss told me that as we hadn't used them for 30 years or so to cart them down to the furnace and they went in with other scrap to cast ploughshares.

He explained the demise of cast iron panels from the balconies of so many country hotels:

> Its main problem was that it was too heavy—it outlasted the wood and when the wooden handrail or flooring rotted it became dangerous and could fall out. To reset the panels often meant that a lot of the woodwork would have to be replaced as well, so it was usually taken down and sold as scrap.

The Queensland Style—wood, lace and shade.

Brisbane was established as a penal settlement in 1825 and was not opened to free settlers until February 1842 when the order proclaiming the Moreton Bay district a penal settlement was finally rescinded.

The popular notion of the wide verandahed house raised off the ground on metal capped wooden stumps is now a trademark of Queensland, but this unique form of vernacular domestic architecture did not appear until the mid 1870s. Old photographs show most Queensland verandahs to be bordered by wood until the 1870s when decorative iron also came into use.

On 20 May 1882 the *Queenslander* published an article 'The Iron Foundries of Brisbane'. In wordy Victorian prose it gives us a clearer picture of the names and output of Brisbane's foundries at that period than we have of the industry in Sydney and Melbourne. However only passing attention is given to 'the ornamental and durable castings now made for verandah and balcony railings and supports that have grown in favour so rapidly during the past few years'.[12]

The *Queenslander* estimated that there were over 360 men busily employed in Brisbane's foundries and listed the largest as being Messrs. Smith, Forrester, and Co., 'recently passed from the hands of Messrs R. R. Smellie & Co., into those of the present occupants, is the oldest, and, it would not be considered invidious to say, the most complete foundry in this city'.[13]

Here the reader is given a tantalisingly brief glimpse of the 'pattern makers' shop', where colonial craftsmen carved and sometimes designed 'in wood the exact counterpart of every casting that has to be made, and here five men and two apprentices are kept busily employed'. Additional

attention is paid to the more spectacular process of pouring the molten iron into mouldings of massive rollers for sugar mills and railway and mining plant.

Other 'temples of Vulcan' are visited, including the foundry of Mr Richard Godfrey & Sons, of Montague Street, South Brisbane and formerly of Victoria, where cast iron decoration was all the rage. Mr Godfrey specialised in ornamental work and 'has brought about 300 patterns with him, besides which, being himself a pattern-maker he is able to give effect to any design that may be brought to him ... some of which are of really elegant design and calculated to foster the growing taste for this description of house decoration'.[14]

The *Queenslander* misspells Harvey Sargeant & Co., as Messrs Harvey, Sergeant & Co. A small foundry established in 1882, they were more accurately described as 'having a great variety of balcony mountings, including some handsome patterns which had been reproduced with great sharpness and exactness'.[15]

This foundry was to design and manufacture some extraordinary Australian patterns, and was the only one of the seven mentioned to register its designs.

The first registration for copyright in Queensland was made by J. Crase and A. T. Rees on 13.11.1885, being the same design registered by A. T. Rees in New South Wales two years earlier, *NSW 132*, on 6.9.1883. Other New South Wales designs of A. T. Rees were registered in partnership with J. Crase and the first original Queensland design, a bracket *Qld 17*, was the ninth registration made in the state and submitted by Harvey Sargeant & Co., on 1.9.1886.

The John Crase & Co. Foundry, after a succession of partnerships, was still operating in Brisbane at the turn of the century and made the last Queensland registration for decorative ironwork, *Qld 186*, on 7.11.1902. A catalogue from this foundry, *John Crase & Co., New Book of Designs of Ironwork*, with no date but probably produced in the first few years of this century, is held in the John Oxley Library in Brisbane and some of its

Top From the early twentieth century Brisbane foundry catalogue of John Crase & Co., *New Book of Designs of Ironwork*.

Bottom This shady wood and iron balcony and verandah at 109 Gregory Terrace, Brisbane, uses a familiar Queensland design from the John Crase & Co. catalogue.

Left Crase's ironwork on the Cafe Royal, which is now Brisbane's Hotel Carlton. John Crase & Co.'s decorative ironwork is seen all over Queensland.

Right Deep shade-giving wooden friezes are a feature of Brisbane's houses and hotels. The design on the balcony panels of the three-storey Regatta Hotel at Toowong was registered by H. Sargeant & Co. *Qld 19* on 7.9.1886.

Some tropical Queensland verandahs are screened only by wood.

H. Sargeant & Co., rare balusters featuring the kangaroo, emu and aboriginal hunters and the equally rare bracket with the kangaroo, emu and a tendril sprouting the rose, shamrock and thistle. The balusters were removed from a Brisbane house prior to its demolition and are now in storage.

original and elaborate designs are easily recognised throughout Queensland, from Warwick in the south to Townsville and Charters Towers in the tropical north. The catalogue shows a picture of the Cafe Royal in Queen Street Brisbane in 1894 or 1895 with the caption 'Specimens of Ironwork Cast by *John Crase & Co.*'. The Cafe Royal became the Metropole Hotel and later, with an added storey, the Carlton Hotel, a Brisbane landmark, and one of the finest inner city iron lace hotel facades in Australia to have escaped the wrecker's hammer.

Unfortunately no catalogue of H. Sargeant & Co. seems to have survived. On 9.5.1887, possibly in anticipation of the centenary of Australia's foundation seven months later, this foundry registered four unique and original patterns: three balusters and one bracket. The central baluster features a kangaroo and an emu beside a tree fern, flanked by two facing Aboriginal hunters armed with spears on narrower balusters. The balusters have the maker's name, *Harvey Sargeant & Co.*, cast into the panels, which is unusual in Australian decorative iron work. The panels are prob-

Top right 'Ay Ot Look-out' at Charters Towers was built in the 1890s using balusters, *above*, which can be seen in the John Crase & Co. catalogue (see page 172).

Below Southerners often mistake the roof ventilator, such as this one on a 1909 house in Charters Towers, for a chimney.

ably the rarest items of all decorative architectural Australiana. The balusters have only been sighted once in Brisbane, and the brackets once in Melbourne, where Mr B. Macgregor of Armadale rescued them from a house in Queenscliff where they were about to be 'carted off to the tip.' The brackets *opposite* feature a tendril from which is sprouting what were then accepted as the symbols of Australia's origins, the rose, thistle and shamrock.

The Queensland tropical house on wooden stilts, often with a modest skirt of woodwork draped in front of them and a belt of cast iron around its shady verandah, is usually given scant attention in books on Australian architecture. Yet it is one of the most distinctively Australian styles of housing, superbly adapted to the climate: a wet season when the rain comes down in bucketfuls and humid nights when the verandah can be used as an airy sleep out. However, they have not become fashionable, as have terrace houses in southern states, and are being bulldozed by developers at an alarming rate.

Australia's Iron Lace

Townsville in the early 1900s had a number of three-storey iron lace hotels, as well as the Municipal Buildings (page 92) which before their demolition in the 1970s, had the longest iron lace facade in Australia.

Queenslanders spend a lot of their leisure
time on their verandahs, which can be
screened for privacy with lattice or blinds.

The only iron on many of these wooden houses is the galvanised iron roof, and the ventilator—which southerners often mistake for a chimney. Many have a semi-circular or triangular pediment over the entrance with a fretworked floral motif in hardwood. This decorative woodwork overwhelms the iron on many tropical Queensland houses. J. & J. Rooney & Co. was one of Queensland's leading building firms during the final decades of the last century. They also manufactured pre-cut wooden brackets, fanlights and columns, which like cast iron decoration, could be ordered by architects and builders. In Maryborough and Rockhampton the delicacy of the cast iron decoration is rivalled by the dainty patterns fretworked in hardwood which accompany it—these are worthy of a book in themselves.

Verandahs are important in tropical Queensland and are an extension of the living area. People may spend as much time on their verandah in summer as within the rooms of the house. They add an informal and

Above The tropical sun casts a shadowy web on the floor of the bandstand in Anzac Park, Townsville. The balusters are a Queensland registration, *Qld 83*, by John Crase & Co. on 7.2.1889.

Above right Tattersall's Hotel, Townsville, was built by J. & J. Rooney, who often used this pattern, originally from the catalogue of the Saracen Foundry, Glasgow (see page 173).

Below right Buchanan's Hotel, before the tragic fire in 1982.

friendly touch to a house and can be screened with blinds or wooden lattice work to provide shade, privacy and coolness. Verandah columns are invariably wooden in domestic architecture but round cast iron columns were sometimes used on hotels and public buildings. Two patterns of open grillework columns were registered for copyright but are rarely seen.

Turn of the century photographs show Townsville in North Queensland to be lavishly decorated with iron lace. A number of three-storey hotels, had they survived, would rival those of the *vieux carré* in New Orleans. The Municipal Building, which included the Central Hotel, had a continuous iron balcony which extended for over 240 metres and was the longest iron lace facade in Australia. This was demolished during the early 1970s; had Townsville's iron lace buildings survived the demolitions and fires its architecture would attract as many tourists as do the beautiful islands nearby on the Great Barrier Reef.

Townsville's triple-storey Buchanan's Hotel was opened in 1902

Municipal Buildings, Townsville.

The Municipal Buildings in Flinders Street, Townsville (before their demolition during the 1970s) had the longest iron lace facade in Australia.

adorned by a flamboyant veil of both cast and wrought iron, which according to local historian Mrs Dorothy Gibson-Wilde, was manufactured locally by Green's Foundry. The deep wrought-iron fringes contained coloured glass inserts and the frontage was undoubtedly the most extraordinary display of iron lace in Australia.

A tragic fire late in 1982 destroyed the wooden rear section of the hotel but left the brick frontage and its ironwork 'with limited damage' but still intact. In a panic move the local council started demolishing the rear section and, despite frantic efforts of the National Trust, later demolished the elegant frontage at night. The next day the stunned citizens of Townsville learnt that the council was worried that falling debris could have interrupted traffic! Local architect and National Trust representative Mr Graham Knott states that he had successfully restored bomb damaged buildings in London that were more severely damaged than Buchanan's.

Some of Townsville's happier surviving hotels are the Great Northern (1900), Tattersall's (c. 1899) and the Australian (1888). The latter hotel has a baluster pattern which is unique to North Queensland but of unknown provenance. Tattersall's Hotel was built by the Queensland building firm J. & J. Rooney and made extensive use of the cross pattern shown on page 91 on many of their other buildings in North Queensland. This design can also be seen in the 1882 edition of Walter Macfarlane's Saracen

Buchanan's Hotel in 1905, a few years after its opening.

Foundry catalogue (Glasgow), as well as the 1887 Fulton's Foundry catalogue (Adelaide). As the castings on the balcony of Tattersall's Hotel do not carry the Saracen Foundry trademark, it is likely that they are locally made copies.

Maryborough, on the banks of the Mary River, 250 kilometres to the north of Brisbane has an exceptionally fine collection of Queensland-style houses elaborately decorated with timber and cast iron. Until recently it also had a traditional foundry which was still producing cast iron panels of its own regional design.

Australia's Iron Lace

The elaborate iron lace verandah of the Imperial Hotel stands above the wild fruit trees and abandoned gardens of Ravenswood. Built in 1902 and still owned and run by the Delaney family, the Imperial is under a National Trust preservation order.

The 'Crown of Thorns' pattern on Sterling, an 1883 Maryborough house.

Maryborough iron lace patterns.

Mr Bob Daniels was a foundryman for 50 years in the foundry established by his father in 1909. The foundry closed on his retirement in December 1981 and in its final years was again producing cast iron baluster panels as a stock item for house renovators. Mr Daniels recalled:

My father produced most of the post-1909 iron lace that was used in the Maryborough district but my first job as a youngster in the early days of the depression was breaking it up after we'd bought it as scrap and putting it back in the furnace. The mainstay of my foundry was cast iron woodburning stoves—the Scotia—we'd been exporting them for years when a government bloke showed up, Department of Export Incentive or something, to encourage exports, and he was amazed when I told him we'd already shipped over 2000 overseas.

There was nothing complicated about our methods—we used traditional methods and commonsense. We used the same coke-burning furnace my father built in 1909 and usually used all scrap iron instead of buying pig iron. For the moulds we used a local sandy loam which contained a light clay bond—we never had to treat it other than to add water and coal dust—a couple of truck loads of it would do us for a year. I even used to repair the furnace with it mixed with fire clay.

In the last few years I received so many enquiries for iron lace panels that I started making them again—I used some original Maryborough panels as patterns, I call this one the *crown of thorns* (above) and we sold hundreds before we closed down.

I've never had time for technocrats—we only ever used traditional methods. We'd make the moulds, I'd fire the furnace, we'd pour the castings and then go home. Nothing romantic about it—it was also damned hard work.

'Crown of Thorns' balusters on the balcony of a deserted store in Ravenswood.

Townsville lace. The Great Northern Hotel, built in 1900 and The Australian Hotel, built 1888 with Queensland lace work of unknown origin.

Nothing can match Australian colonial lace. I can pick the aluminium imitation stuff a mile off—it's very thin and will turn to powder. Genuine cast iron lasts for generations.

Unfortunately no buyers could be found for Mr. Daniels' foundry when he reached retirement age, even though he had more orders for iron lace panels than he could fill.

The 'Crown of Thorns' pattern can also be seen in Ravenswood, near Charters Towers in North Queensland. Now almost deserted, the town is remarkable for the two surviving pubs and the closed and empty stores which still flaunt the 'goldfields brash' style of the turn of the century when vast amounts of gold were being extracted from the quartz reefs below.

The most northern point cast iron decoration reached on the Australian continent was Cooktown, whose confident founders must have thought that the gold from the Palmer River fields would last forever. They imported building materials from the south at enormous expense to build their imposing banks and offices.

Tiny Croydon, in Queensland's isolated Gulf country, also once had a population of many thousands during its former gold rich days. A few remaining frills of iron lace can be seen screwed to the verandahs of some of the long-deserted houses and the remains of its foundry are scattered with pieces of broken scrap iron and the crumbling brickwork of the furnace.

The Palace Hotel, one of Perth's few remaining gold boom hotels. Its prime position in St George's Terrace made it a candidate for demolition but it is now to be incorporated into the skyscraper which will rise above it.

Cast iron decoration arrived late in Western Australia, after the heyday of its use in New South Wales and Victoria, and, as in Queensland, was used well into the twentieth century. Some pockets of iron lace terrace houses still exist in Perth and Fremantle; however they were never popular with the inhabitants of the former Swan River Colony who preferred to call their streets 'terraces' and their terrace houses 'tenements'. Local architectural historian, Ian Molyneux, in conversations with elderly residents records that the 'tenements' were usually looked down upon by all.

In some of Perth's older areas, such as Subiaco, there is more 'wooden lace', if it can be called that, than cast iron. Local jarrah was fretworked into elegant patterns to adorn the verandah columns of turn of the century bungalows built with the rich red bricks so characteristic of Perth's houses. Subiaco's wooden verandah decoration is similar to the decorative woodwork seen in Maryborough and other Queensland towns.

Perth 'boomed' in the mid 1890s when, in a reversal of fortunes, the eastern colonies were in a moribund state of depression. Gold discoveries in the waterless scrub 600 kilometres to the east of Perth in 1892 and 1893 turned Western Australia into Australia's richest gold producer. Building surged forward in Perth, much of it in the opulent high Victorian style of lavish ornamentation in plaster and iron that the economic depression had halted in the east.

Some fine iron lace balconied hotels were built in Perth during this period and were demolished 80 years later in another boom of speculative high rise development during the 1970s. The Swan River frontage hotels

These early twentieth century terraces in Catherine Street, Subiaco, are distinguished by the distinctive palmette design on their balconies and the West Australian emblem of the black swan stuccoed on a pediment in the centre of the row.

were demolished and replaced with high rise office blocks for a new generation of mining companies.

The Palace Hotel survived many threats of demolition and managed to stay intact on its prime site, even though finer examples such as the Federal Hotel fell victim to the developers' bulldozers. Perhaps it was remorse or nostalgia for their vanished pubs which caused such resentment among the citizens of Perth who have insisted that the Palace Hotel be retained and incorporated into the skyscraper being constructed above it.

The palmette design on the balcony of the Palace Hotel can also be seen on the old Perth Fire Brigade Station and on a row of 1904 terraces in Catherine Street, Subiaco. The pattern appears as No. 70 (see page 175) in the 1887 edition of the *Illustrated Catalogue of Fulton's Castings*, Adelaide. The Fulton pattern has almost identical dimensions to the same pattern in the 1882 edition of the Saracen Foundry, Glasgow, catalogue (see page 173), from where the Adelaide foundry either purchased the design or copied it using an imported casting. It also appears in slightly larger dimensions as No. 597 in the 1897 "Sun" Foundry catalogue (see page 177), Adelaide. This pattern is more common in Perth than in Adelaide where it has only been seen once.

The Catherine Street terraces were decrepit in the 1970s with only a couple of the original panels left in place. Vaughan's Castings Pty Ltd, using the originals as patterns, cast reproduction panels for the restorers. The terraces carry the West Australian symbol of the black swan stuccoed on the parapet which, together with its rare lacework, gives these once despised 'tenements' two of the most original exterior features to be seen on any twentieth century Australian house.

The sunflower pattern is common in Victoria on boom era houses and hotels.

This house at 79 South Street, Fremantle, has all the components of domestic Australian iron—galvanised and cast, both decorative and functional.

Iron lace can be seen on West Australian buildings from Albany on King Georges Sound on the Southern Ocean, to Broome in the north and Meekatharra and Kalgoorlie in the interior. Most of the designs appear in the two mentioned Adelaide catalogues and it seems likely that the bulk of it was supplied from Adelaide until Metters Ltd, an Adelaide foundry, is known to have established a foundry in Perth in the early twentieth century.

Woodbridge, now owned by the National Trust, is the finest domestic building in Western Australia and is situated at Guilford on the upper reaches of the Swan River overlooking newly planted vineyards. Woodbridge was built for parliamentarian and newspaper proprietor Charles Harpur during 1884–85 and is one of the few colonial mansions with documentation on its imported ironwork, though ironically some of the ironwork itself is missing. Among Harpur's papers in the Battye Library in Perth are invoices from a firm in England for the supply of an ornamental balcony with 24 columns on the verandah and twenty on the balcony. Together with a spiral staircase which is still in use the total cost was £250. Harpur also ordered his parquetry flooring from England, which was dispatched in zinc lined cases and cost £39.19.0.

Harpur's records show that in October 1884 his architect and builder had two foremen working on the site, and under them were 23 carpenters, four plasterers, a blacksmith, three painters, nine labourers, three apprentices, one bricklayer and two iron workers. They worked a nine and a half hour day and were paid from 1/- to 1/4d per hour.

The hollow cast iron columns on Woodbridge also serve as downpipes from the roof guttering. The original imported balusters were lost during World War Two, when the balcony and verandah were enclosed and the building was converted to a convalescent home for elderly ladies. Woodbridge was transferred to the National Trust and work started on its restoration in 1968, the year prior to the demolition of Perth's Federal Hotel. The Trust was fortunate in acquiring the Adelaide-made balusters from the Federal's double balconies and installed them on Woodbridge. A superb restoration was carried out and the house was opened to the public in 1970.

Charles Harpur's extensive papers in the Battye Library in Perth show that he paid £1/4/6 per 1000 for the richly coloured red bricks to build Woodbridge. The hollow cast iron columns drain rain water from the guttering and were imported from England in 1883. The iron balusters are from the Federal Hotel, demolished in 1969.

3

Decline and Depression

Sydney in the 1890s. A man and his dog, down on their luck, on the steps of the 'Door of Hope' Mission.

The city grinds the owners of the faces in the street
Henry Lawson, July 1888

Sydney architect, John Barlow, loved to alliterate but deplored iron lace terraces—among other things they gave him indigestion. He wrote of them in 1892 'with their hideous iron balconies and preposterous parapets ... pitiful in their vulgarity, dispirited, dyspeptic'.[16]

A few years earlier in 1886, a colleague in Melbourne, J. B. de Libra, heaped abuse on the confectionery tastes of some Melbourne architects:

> The height of some ambitions must surely be to besmatter a facade with so-called ornament much as a perverted ingenuity does that direst of human perpetrations—the bride-cake[17]

Nor were engineers at a loss for words 'there is a term' wrote one in 1892, with a touch of Thurber, '"cast-iron impudence" ...... with its origins in the glaring and impudent manner in which cast-iron ornament is plastered over our buildings'.[18]

It is not surprising that a fashion which had gone to such extremes would have its critics and a limited life span, but while cast iron decoration remained the delight of the working and middle classes and was still in favour with their wealthier clients as well, architects did not make their scathing attacks on it publicly. Criticism of its use, and of overembellishment of all kinds, was mostly kept within the pages of architectural and building journals.

When British and American architects began to champion the idea of the 'garden suburb', the fashion filtered through to Sydney and Melbourne. With their expanding transport systems and seemingly limitless space for urban development, the previously popular terraces with their frills and embellishment very suddenly became unacceptable, and a bungalow in a leafy suburb connected to the city by tram or rail became the mode.

The Sydney hardware store F. Lassetter & Co. issued a mail order catalogue which still advertised cast iron panels as late as 1914. The top right-hand panel (*No. MI 493*) in this page from their 1911 catalogue, sold for two shillings and ninepence per foot and was the first pattern to be registered in New South Wales—on 1879—by D. Livingstone 32 years earlier. The date of registration of a pattern is not a reliable guide to the age of a building on which it is found. Some panels may have the name of a foundry and a date but this is usually the date of the pattern's registration, not the date of manufacture.

The change was rapid, only twelve years separate Barlow's dyspepsia from the popular notion expressed by visiting Englishman James Inglis in *Our Australian Cousins* in 1880 'even the less pretentious structures bear many marks of taste, and an advanced state of embellishment'.[19] He believed that the material prosperity within was as high as the external embellishment implied—which was exactly the message such decoration meant to convey.

There was not a distinct cut off point for the popularity of cast iron in Australia. It continued to be used on the verandahs of country hotels well into the twentieth century; the Sydney hardware emporium of F. Lassetter & Co., advertised baluster panels in their catalogue until 1914. Panels must have been available also from country foundries as the Criterion Hotel in Warwick, Queensland (see page 129), had its iron balcony, of a Queensland pattern, installed in 1917 and the Victoria Hotel in Dimboola in the western districts of Victoria is an iron lace pub, built along traditional lines, with the year 1924 on the parapet (see page 132). A row of double-

Australia's Iron Lace

Restored terraces at Randwick and below, Westgate Terrace, Ruthven Street, Bondi Junction built in 1893. '... Even the less pretentious structures bear many marks of taste, and an advanced state of embellishment' wrote visiting Englishman James Inglis of Sydney in 1880. 'Preposterous parapets' and 'Cast iron impudence' thundered architects only twelve years later.

storey terraces with iron balconies was built in Lithgow, New South Wales in 1919.

But the heyday of its use in the eastern cities finished abruptly in the grim economic depression of the mid 1890s when areas such as Sydney's Paddington, and Carlton and Fitzroy in Melbourne where it was used most lavishly, also slid from fashion to disrepute with the changing aesthetics of the new century.

Henry Lawson is remembered most for his short stories and poems about the outback but he spent most of his adult life in Sydney. *'Dossing Out'* and *'Camping'* was written during the 1890s depression; Lawson surveyed the city streets one rainy night and counted over 200 unfortunates who had been driven from the Domain and the parks to sleep on the asphalt pavement under the verandahs of York Street.

> There is no prison like the city for a poor man. Nearly every man the traveller meets in the bush is about as dirty and ragged as himself, and just about as hard up; but in the city nearly every man the poor unemployed meets is a dude, or at least, well dressed, and the unemployed *feels* dirty and mean and degraded by the contrast—and despised.[20]

The 1890s are thought to have been a vigorous decade in Australia with a surge in literature and art that expressed a distinctly Australian point of view. Yet two thirds of the population lived in towns and cities and were far from being the rugged legendary figures from a Banjo Paterson ballad or a Furphy novel. In Michael Cannon's classic social history *Life in the Cities* it takes a strong stomach to accompany him through the pages where he describes how the poor lived and worked—especially the ten- and twelve-year-old children working in slaughterhouses.

Many of the houses built during boom times were thrown up by jerry-builders and 'land sweaters'. They became slums even as they were finished, with impossibly cramped rooms, and balconies that reached out over narrow undrained streets. Other terrace houses were built to last, as time has shown, in areas respectable enough for the landlord developer to wish to live, usually in a more grandiose house in the centre of his row and lease the others. Even these did not have long to wait before they were also regarded as slum areas. During the late 1890s, with the new concept of the garden suburb attracting them, the middle classes abandoned the inner city terrace houses in droves, leaving only the poor to live in the outrageously decorated and increasingly decrepit terraces. Many of the more amply proportioned houses were turned into 'residentials' where the tenants sublet rooms, sometimes the maid's room from days of former affluence, to lodgers. By the 1920s Paddington in Sydney had acquired such a sleazy reputation that the expression 'a room, in a reso, in Paddo' meant that to be living in one was to have hit the rock bottom of one's luck.

In his book *Faces of the Street*, a photographic and sociological survey of Sydney's William Street just prior to its widening in 1916, Max Kelly estimates that as many as fifteen to twenty per cent of metropolitan Sydney's adult population was living as boarders or lodgers at this period.[21] To 'take in a lodger' was commonplace in many working class areas until as late as the end of World War Two and was often an indispensable part of a household economy. In Ruth Park's *Harp in the South* written in 1947, the Darcy family in their once grand, but now appallingly dilapidated terrace at 12½ Plymouth Street 'smelling of leaking gas, and rats and mouldering wallpaper', let two attic rooms to lodgers for seven

These solid mid-century terraces in William Street, Sydney were being used as residentials when photographed in 1916. The notice in the window of number 181 says 'Vacancy', with a sign on the door 'Welcome', and on the balcony one of the lodgers advertises 'Costumiere'. (*City of Sydney Council*)

shillings and sixpence per week. The 1920s saw another building surge in Sydney—more houses were built in that decade than had been in any previous one as more people left the inner city for the new suburbs. The 'bride-cake' terraces in the inner city, like Miss Havesham's wedding cake in *Great Expectations*, sagged and mouldered. An alert 85 year old Mrs Irene Mores recalled street life in 1909 in Sydney's Redfern, with *Sydney Morning Herald* journalist Susan Malloy in 1982:

> Forty cramped terraces ranged on each side, bounded by Caroline Street at the top and Vine Street at the bottom. Their balconies, overhanging the absurdly narrow footpaths and linked with iron lace, clung to each other to meet the downward grade.
>
> The division of the lane was not only a physical one. Certain unwritten laws pertained to social life there. There was 'the top' and 'the bottom'.
>
> My home at the top was one of a group of four identical houses with glazed stone faces, creamy in colour, their doorways and sills picked out in a deep shade of russet. The doors of finely grained wood were polished and replete with iron knockers and brass letter slots.
>
> Each day began with the sloshing of the houses' sills with buckets of water. This cleaned away the sooty factory outfall. Footpaths glistened in the early morning sunshine, and when the council water-cart added its glitter to the roadway, the stage was set for the day's drama.
>
> The postmen and rent-collectors banged knockers from top to bottom. The rabbit man yodelled 'brer-rabbit-rabbit-O' as he made his way along

Hard times and bare feet in Balfour Street in the inner Sydney suburb of Chippendale in 1909.

Street urchins pose for the camera of the Sydney Council photographer as he photographs these jerry built terraces before their demolition in 1909. The little boy on the far right lacks the bravado of the others.

the street with a small cart and undersized horse. While mother selected the best of the rabbits slung across the bars of the cart at nine pence a pair, I held the plate high.

I flinched as the head was hatchetted, the pelt skilfully peeled off, and turned away as it lay naked and bleeding, its furry paws folded in meek submission. There were 'ribs only' for those who could not afford a whole rabbit.

A good meal could be made with the addition of waste vegetables—outsize cabbage leaves and such, salvaged from the markets and brought home in billy-carts.

At the end of the day a sickly street lamp lit the stage for each night's unpredictable drama. Invariably, arranged fights took place at the lanes. These were interrupted regularly by one of two sounds—the cops' whistle or the strains of an accordian (of the City Mission). In either case it was 'all off till later'.

'Preposterous parapets' at Oxford Street, Bondi Junction. Richly glazed tiles, Moorish arches and classical busts—some retain traces of their original paintwork—but the section on the right has been painted an unimaginative brown.

This row of terraces on the corner of Palmer and St Peters Streets, East Sydney, was being demolished in 1922. Such items as fireplaces, windows and doors are being salvaged for resale but the ironwork from the cantilevered balconies was then unfashionable and has probably been sold as scrap.

Two rival gangs of children and one dog glare at each other and ignore photographer Harold Cazneaux in a Surry Hills street in 1911. (*Art Gallery of New South Wales. Gift of the Cazneaux family*)

... at any hour of the night violence would erupt. Often half-clothed men and women brawled in drunken stupor. The ill-lit alleyway echoed their screams and abusive language; the crash of crockery, as kitchens were wrecked; and beer bottles flung in rage smashed on the asphalt. An excitement-hungry crowd surged on the scene only to be dispersed by the whistle of the cops as they came in to break up the melée.[22]

Mrs Etta Turner from her hospital bed recalled the tough days of her childhood in the streets of Paddington:

We didn't have any real affection for the terrace we lived in. Why should we? We were only paying rent to a landlord for it like everyone else in the street, and our landlords were the Church of England. And the iron lace, well, we never really thought about it. It was always just there. Our loyalty was to the family and to the street—or at least our end of the street. 'Get back to yer own end!' we'd say to kids that strayed up our end. We'd only shop at the corner shop at our end of the street, never at the other one.

The double-storey terraces in the street of her slum childhood now carry huge price tags. Owners are spending thousands more on highlighting the elements of their exuberant Victorian decoration and are becoming used to camera laden tourists visiting their suburb.

Not all terrace house areas have undergone this startling revival of popularity and values. In parts of Redfern frightened Vietnamese and Aboriginal faces peer out of the windows of the same terraces that housed poor Irish immigrants a hundred years ago. They are suspicious of the camera at first and have to be reassured that the photograph is not for a real estate advertisement. 'Why do you want to photograph this rusty old

Top A row of 1885 terrace houses in Randwick, Sydney.

Above A row of restored early twentieth-century terraces in George Street, East Fremantle, West Australia.

stuff?' a young Aboriginal boy asked me from his sagging balcony.

Many terrace balconies were enclosed during the depression to provide an extra makeshift bedroom and the lacework removed and sold for scrap. Often the houses still face the street, like a face that has replaced its smile with a frown of fibro or wood.

The Housing Investigation Boards of Victoria (1938) and New South Wales (1941) deplored the state of inner city areas of Melbourne and Sydney which in some cases had been little changed since the 1890s. Most terrace houses, they found, were in an abject state of disrepair and concluded that they were a blight to the eye, beyond renovation, unfit to live in and 'entirely sub-standard'. The only answer was 'demolition and replacement'. Both states formed Housing Commissions and after World War Two parts of inner Melbourne were levelled and high-rise flats, twenty storeys high, were constructed.

In Sydney the Housing Commission developed large housing estates in the western suburbs. The decaying inner city terraces awaited their fate; town planners had passed sentence on most of inner Sydney in no uncertain terms. The Cumberland County Planning Scheme of 1948 designated a ring of suburbs close to the city, comprising Paddington, Annandale, Balmain, Glebe and Wolloomooloo as 'obsolete areas in which immediate demolition of buildings is considered necessary' or as areas in which 'buildings should be replaced within the next twenty five years'.[23]

How the planners were confounded and their plans reversed is a remarkable story.

4

The Country Pub
Verandah

*Sydney has eight hundred taverns; which plainly
demonstrates the bibulous propensities of the
inhabitants.*

W. *Shaw* Land of Promise *1854*

Many other visitors to Sydney were awed by both the number of public-
houses and by the prodigious amount of liquor consumed by the colonists.

The unwilling immigrants of the First Fleet, convicts, marines,
officers and a handful of gentry, also brought with them a thirst for the
appallingly adulterated mix of spirits they called grog or rum. The corrupt
opportunists among the officers of the New South Wales Corps were
quick to capitalise on the 'bibulous propensities' of the convicts and
settlers by gaining a monopoly of the supply and sale of spirits.

When Captain William Bligh RN arrived to take over the gov-
ernorship of the colony in August 1806 he was horrified and astounded by
the bizarre trade in rum and the power of the military men who had con-
trol of its supply. One of his biggest squabbles with John Macarthur
occurred when he seized a 60-gallon still imported by Macarthur and
ordered that it be impounded until it could be shipped back to England.
When Bligh was arrested by an inebriated contingent of the New South
Wales Corps in January 1808 the power struggle which ensued led to yet
another mutiny in his career, and has been appropriately called the Rum
Rebellion.

In his book *Settlers and Convicts* Alexander Harris is thought to have
fictionalised some of his experiences, but as something of a reformed sin-
ner himself, his descriptions of life in New South Wales in the 1830s are
invaluable. Harris described a visit to a grog shop which must have been
typical of many:

> ... an old dilapidated place, properly enough called 'The Sheer Hulk', which
> had been deprived of its licence on account of the practices and characters
> admitted by its landlord; it was, however, still occupied, and as the occupier

The Windsor, a gold boom hotel in South
Perth, wears a dainty cast iron facade. The
design on the balcony panels appears in the
1897 edition of the "Sun" Foundry
catalogue (page 177).

Coyle's Clubhouse Hotel at Hill End, New South Wales, built in the 1870s. Like the nearby Royal Hotel it has a French pattern on its balcony although it was installed upside down. (Compare with page 57.) (*Mitchell Library*)

In this 1887 architectural drawing of a hotel to be built in Forest Lodge, Sydney, the architect borrowed elements from different patterns to compose his balustrade design. (*New South Wales Government Printer*)

was no longer under the apprehension of losing his licence, the scenes displayed nightly were of tenfold worse character than ever.[24]

Charles Corbyn wrote on Sydney's taverns in a much lighter note a decade later. Corbyn was an irreverent court reporter of the 1850s who with great wit and gusto—and a complete disregard for the libel laws—amused the readers of his weekly column in *Bell's Life in Sydney* with his reporters on the antics and repartee he witnessed in court. Corbyn loved to sharpen his wits on lawyers, police, magistrates and prisoners alike as well as tipsy gold diggers who were before the bench for causing 'a general scrimmage' or a 'breach of the peace' at the Help-me-through-the-world tavern at Darlinghurst or The Currency Lass in Pitt Street.

The Sheer Hulk, the Help-me-through-the-world and other colourful pub names such as the Green Man, Foul Anchor, Crooked Billet, Hawkesbury Settler and the Red Cow have disappeared from Sydney. Victorian and New South Wales gold towns had a large quota of Brian Boru, Shamrock, Harp of Erin and Home Rule hotels for the thirsty and political Irish, and the Hobart waterfront had appropriate pub names such as the Whale Fishery and the Calcutta. Less endearing names were the Blacksnake Inn and Greenhide Mary's Wine Saloon in western New South Wales.

Many of Sydney's first grog shops were no doubt as insidious as the Sheer Hulk but a glance through Joseph Fowles' *Sydney in 1848* shows respectable looking hotels such as Thomas Murphy's Adelphi Hotel and

Above The Victoria Hotel at Rutherglen, Victoria, wears a familiar Victorian pattern which features a sunflower.

Middle The Richmond Arms Hotel, Richmond, Tasmania, has a baluster pattern first registered in Victoria *Vic 158* on 30.12.1875.

Below The Royal Hotel at Hill End, New South Wales, built in 1872. The balcony pattern can be seen in the Parisian catalogue of *Barbezat et Cie* (see page 57).

Right Another Royal Hotel, this one at Bathurst, has its initial R as the central motif in the balcony panels.

Opposite top The Royal Hotel at the turn of the century.

Opposite bottom The Royal today bearing the scars of 'modernisation' is to be restored.

Squatter's Arms, a double-storey hotel in York Street and John Sparke's five-storeyed Royal Hotel.

Inns and half-way houses opened as roads spread inland from Sydney and Melbourne. Charles Darwin on a brief excursion to Bathurst from Sydney in 1836 stayed at the Weatherboard Inn at what is now Wentworth Falls and at the Blackheath Inn, 'a very comfortable inn, kept by an old soldier, and it reminded me of the small inns in North Wales'.

Some of the loveliest early roadside inns are in Tasmania where the climate is closer to that of England. As verandahs were not required for shade the inns retained clean and harmonious Georgian lines.

John Pascoe Fawkner, one of the co-founders of Melbourne, had previously run the Cornwall Hotel in Launceston. When the abstemious publican arrived on the banks of the Yarra, he erected a prefabricated building and opened Melbourne's first tavern. He later built a more substantial hotel on the corner of Collins and Market Streets which also served as a lending library.

Gold, and later the spread of the railway system led to the style of the verandahed country pub which overseas visitors regard as being so characteristically Australian, but Australians tend to take for granted. By the 1860s life had settled down on the largest of the goldfields to the business of mining the deep leads. The canvas and stringybark shanties began to disappear and the classic goldfield hotels such as the Royal at Hill End and

the Gold Mines Hotel at Bendigo began to rise above the mullock heaps. The Gold Mines Hotel at the head of Ironbark Gully, (page 130), was built in 1857 and remodelled to its present state a few years later. The beautiful interior and the rosewood and mahogany furnishings have been maintained. The dainty exterior lace work of the balcony panels has an overlapping circles-and-floral motif. It was one of the earliest designs to be registered in Victoria, *Vic. 8*, on 4.5.1870 by J. Lyster and C. Cooke.

One of the Royal's competitors at Hill End during the 1870s was Coyle's Clubhouse Hotel which, like the Royal, had a French pattern on its balcony, but as can be seen in the Holtermann photograph taken in 1872 (page 117) it was installed upside down (compare with page 57).

Melbourne and Sydney terrace house owners cannot afford to be too chauvinistic about their lace work—country gold centres such as Ballarat and Bendigo in Victoria and Bathurst in New South Wales have lavish

Above left Molong, New South Wales. The pattern on the panels made up into a gate is a variant of one shown in the French catalogue on page 57.

Below left A bandstand in Forbes, New South Wales. The baluster design is familiar in Riverina towns of New South Wales and was probably produced by the Cohoe and Walster Foundry in Junee, established in 1893 and still trading as an engineering firm.

Above right Some unusual decorative ironwork can be seen in Bathurst, New South Wales.

Below right The rare crown design in Nathalia, Victoria. The shamrock, rose and thistle can be seen in the frieze.

decorative iron work, manufactured in their own foundries and used with a delicate and original touch.

Most country foundries used the same patterns that can be seen in the cities but there are some outstanding exceptions. The Royal Hotel at Bathurst, New South Wales, has a monogrammed pattern with its initial 'R' cast into the design. These panels are thought to have been cast at a foundry at Lithgow. The Royal Hotel is now undergoing restoration. Bathurst has other unique patterns shown above. A fringe and bracket design featuring a crown appears in the 1901 Excelsior Foundry catalogue. It is rare in its native Melbourne but Nathalia in northern Victoria has a fine example on a verandah in the main street.

Functional verandahs shielded most country town buildings in the Victorian age and provided a shady collonade along the amply proportioned banks, stores and pubs.

Forbes from the balcony of the Vandenberg Hotel. The tower of the Albion Hotel, which was used to spot the incoming Cobb & Co. coaches, can be seen in the distance.

As railways reached prosperous inland agricultural and grazing centres an impetus was provided for the building of more grandiose hotels at railway junctions where passengers needed to rest overnight before continuing by coach. The Albion at Forbes, New South Wales, is typical of these large country hotels that concentrated on providing good quality accommodation and meals as much as quenching the thirsts of the locals. This hotel was first established during the goldrush and bushranging years of the early 1860s. The present three-storey building with its wide shady balcony and verandahs facing onto two streets was erected between 1889 and 1893 in a style redolent of Victorian respectability and confidence. The railway reached Forbes in 1893 and the Albion's manager would send a coach to the station to bring passengers to the hotel. The roof of the Albion is topped with an iron lace crested tower where a lookout was placed to spot the incoming Cobb & Co. coaches from across the plains; so mine host could have his hotel and staff ready to receive the dusty and thirsty travellers.

The railway made travel more comfortable and an army of commercial travellers toured the prosperous towns taking orders which would then be dispatched by rail. Hence the number of Commercial and Railway hotels in country towns which competed for their business. Large, generously proportioned hotels with wide iron-trimmed balconies and

The Commerical and Shamrock hotels in Rochester, Victoria, built in different centuries but in a similar style. The unusual balustrade pattern on the Shamrock can also be seen in Bendigo where it was probably cast.

verandahs continued to be built throughout Australia until well into the twentieth century.

The monumental Shamrock Hotel in Rochester, Victoria was built in 1911–1912 by a wealthy businessman, Tom McMaster, whose business acumen anticipated the prosperity the new Waranga irrigation scheme would bring to the town. The most impressive feature of this fine hotel is its wide verandah with unusual iron panels on the balcony. The same pattern can be seen in Bendigo where the panels were probably cast. Alongside the Shamrock stands the Commercial, a goldrush style hotel built decades before, when Rochester was on the Cobb & Co. coach run from Deniliquin, in the Riverina in New South Wales, to Bendigo and Melbourne. The Shamrock is much larger but the style of the Commercial is only slightly more ornate than the Shamrock, built in the new century.

Similar hotels with characteristic ornate balconies and verandahs were

The Imperial Hotel in Armidale, New South Wales has an unusual arrangement of three columns, the bases of which bear the maker's name—P. F. Revett, W Maitland.

The Rose Hotel in Bunbury, Western Australia was built in 1865. The remodelled facade, using familiar Adelaide patterns, was added in 1897.

The Exchange Hotel in Gawler, South Australia. The geometrical pattern on its balcony can be seen in the 1887 G. E. Fulton & Co., Adelaide catalogue on page 175.

Above left Dulwich Hill, Sydney, in Edwardian times. The footpaths are arcaded by verandahs, with a phalanx of ironwork above. The balcony on the right has a curved balustrade.

Below left Fremantle, Western Australia, was celebrating the opening of a tramway during the same period. The iron balconies form an unbroken line to the horizon of the picture. The right-hand balcony railing above the printers' sign has elements in the design highlighted in different colours. With the advent of the motor car verandahs disappeared from most Australian cities and were replaced by steel awnings.

Cast iron decoration was used in country centres well into the twentieth century. The Criterion Hotel in Ipswich, Queensland was built in 1917.

built across Australia—the Rose Hotel (c. 1900) in Bunbury in the south west of Western Australia (see page 127) boasts iron work which can be seen in the 1897 catalogue of the "Sun" Foundry in Adelaide. The Imperial Hotel in Beardy Street, Armidale, New South Wales was built in the same style at the same period and has the foundry name cast into its iron columns, *P. F. Revett, W Maitland.*

Verandahs over the footpaths of busy commercial streets were once common in Australian cities as well. In Sydney, Section 267 of the Local Government Act, which allows a council to order the removal of any obstruction on a road or footpath (including verandahs and their supporting posts), was enacted during Edwardian times and street verandahs were entirely removed and replaced with awnings. Adelaide and Melbourne have sensibly preserved many of theirs—single-storey verandahs and their iron columns are still a feature of Carlton.

The benefit of hindsight gives a critic superior wisdom years after an event, but to despise or under rate the recent past, especially during periods of rapid economic development, seems to be a common failing among Australians. Much of Australia's architectural heritage disappeared under the wrecker's hammer during the 1950s and 1960s when 'modernisation' was the popular gospel and conservation issues were rarely raised.

The Gold Mines Hotel, Bendigo, Victoria—one of the prettiest iron lace pubs in Australia. The dainty balcony wears one of the earliest Victorian patterns, *Vic 8* registered by J. Lyster and C. Cooke on 4.5.1870.

In country towns the craze for 'modernisation' was even more urgent. Iron lace pub verandahs supported by kerbside columns reminded townspeople of the 'horse and buggy' days and bridle hitching posts which their new prosperity had supposedly left behind.

In the wool boom during the 1950s the price of wool rose to dizzy heights, country towns were prosperous and many families could afford a car for the first time. Most inland towns have broad streets and previously cars would park parallel to the kerb, but to cope with the increased number of vehicles many town councils introduced angle parking where the vehicle was reversed into the kerb at a 45 degree angle. Sometimes the rear fender of a car bumped the verandah columns which could loosen and bring crashing down a heavy iron panel. An obvious answer would have been to re-align the kerb, especially in towns where the streets were wide. But as a resident of the lovely town of Forbes in the central west of New South Wales explained:

> A lot of this town's iron lace balconies and verandahs were demolished in the late fifties—I was on the council at the time that approved it—the reason given was that they were unsafe but the real underlying reason was that they were unpopular, especially with the shopkeepers, because they looked old fashioned. A lot of townspeople would drive to Orange to do their shopping because they thought it was more modern and up to date, and they wanted Forbes to be the same. At one stage both the Vandenberg and Albion hotel balconies had demolition orders on them because the posts had taken a few knocks and they were considered unsafe.

Australia's Iron Lace

Above The Victoria Hotel, Dimboola was built in 1924 and is probably the most recent of Australia's iron lace pubs.

Middle The Hotel Junee in New South Wales was also built in the twentieth century and has locally cast ironwork from the Cohoe and Walster Foundry, Junee.

Below A fanciful view of the Belle Vue Hotel, Brisbane in 1888.

The Belle Vue in 1972 before its balconies were sheared off. The same panels can be seen on the Yungaba Migrant Hostel at Kangaroo Point, Brisbane. Except for the lower band they are identical to those in the Saracen Foundry, Glasgow catalogue shown on page 174.

Both fortunately survived and Forbes has now gone the full circle. Tourists visit Forbes to take in the echoes of its bushranger and gold rush past and to admire its fine Victorian buildings. The pretentious looking post office, town hall and the Albion Hotel reflect the confidence and post-gold rush prosperity of the late Victorian era. Castlemaine, Beechworth, Ballarat and Bendigo in Victoria and Maryborough in Queensland have also preserved their lacy verandahs and share the same feeling of stolid self-assurance reflected in their buildings erected during Australia's centenary.

Rather than being the curators of Australia's architectural heritage, government bodies have often been among its most savage vandals. One of the most appalling acts of official vandalism was the demolition of the Belle Vue Hotel, a graceful 1886 hotel in the heart of Brisbane.

The Belle Vue had been a familiar landmark in Brisbane before that city saw its first motor car, and housed transit passengers from the passing P & O and Orient Line passenger ships. The building was classified by the National Trust not only on its architectural merit but also because it was part of the first civic precinct to be developed in Brisbane. Ironically, its profile of twin towers was designed to echo that of Parliament House alongside in George Street. The balcony panels on the Belle Vue appear in Macfarlane's Saracen Foundry, Glasgow, catalogue and can also be seen on

Above left The Customs House Hotel in Wharf Street, Maryborough, was built to accommodate passengers who arrived by steamer, prior to the railway reaching the town. The balustrades are a common pattern but the brackets and frieze are unusual.

Below left The Old Colonial Hotel in Rockhampton, Queensland carries the year 1897 on its parapet.

Above right The facade of the Australian Hotel, Cowra, New South Wales is somewhat marred by the out of character modern aluminium panels on the verandah —the sparse pattern and oblong frame immediately identify it as pseudo-antique.

Below right The Coolavin Hotel, Goulburn, New South Wales had its ironwork cast at the local foundry.

the Yungaba Migrant Hostel at Kangaroo Point. Both are single sided and were probably cast locally.

The Queensland State Government acquired the hotel in 1967 and used it to lodge visiting country parliamentarians. In June 1974, after years of neglect, the government sheared off the Belle Vue's most distinctive feature—its double-storey balcony and verandah—leaving the building looking emasculated and drab. Shortly afterwards plans for demolition of the building and development of the site were announced. Despite a long and bitter fight to preserve it most Australians were appalled when the Premier of Queensland ordered its night-time demolition on 24 April 1979. Hundreds of people stood by as demolition machinery smashed the Belle Vue to shards and in nearby Queen Street motorists tooted their horns in protest and shame.

At the time of writing, five years after the demolition of the Belle Vue, the site is still being used as a car park.

5

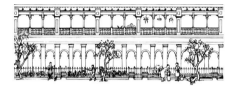

Rebirth and Restoration

Neglected early Sydney ironwork.

Opposite Beautifully restored ironwork at the Agar Steps, in the Rocks area of Sydney.

It will be noted that included in the list (of slum landlords) are the names of members of Parliament, municipal councillors, estate agents, leading business firms, and of well known citizens
Housing Investigation and Slum Abolition Board Report. *(Melbourne) 1936–37: 30*

Paddington is one of the finest examples of totally unplanned urban restoration projects in the world
Tony Wheeler Australia, a travel survival kit 1983:97

After World War Two strident calls for the 'demolition and replacement' of slum areas came from social reformers, politicians, church groups, and, perhaps with less altruistic motives, from builders. It is surprising to us now, with the benefit of hindsight, that renovation, if not restoration, was not seriously cosidered until the early sixties. Even during the thirties, when Melbourne was scandalised with the exposure of some of its most prominent citizens as 'slum landlords', there seems to have been little pressure applied to them to bring their houses up to even a basically acceptable standard. In Sydney, the Glebe Estate of the Church of England owned an enormous number of houses in poor areas where the tenants paid very little in rent but maintenance of the increasingly decrepit houses was negligible.

A critical housing shortage was a major issue in postwar Australia and remained so for many years. Both New South Wales' and Victoria's Housing Commissions seriously underestimated the growth rates of Sydney's and Melbourne's populations. Shortages of bricks, tiles and timber hampered and frustrated owner/builders and on the Housing Commission estates services such as sewerage and kerbing and guttering lagged dismally behind, unable to keep up with the sprawling new suburbs.

The suburban sprawl of Australia's cities gave waspish writers such as Robin Boyd and Allan Ashbolt much to sharpen their wits and writing

Many designs, such as the rare pattern *above left* and the registered design *NSW 92, below left*, have a continuous upper and lower band to give a feeling of flow and continuity. If you are having such a panel recast you should remember that the new panel will have slightly smaller dimensions because of contraction in the casting process.

Right A tiny 'Juliet sized' balcony at the rear of a Paddington terrace.

skills on, but few critics tried to come up with a feasible alternative plan to house urban Australia.

The postwar immigration scheme brought in hundreds of thousands of migrants for whom, in their previous experience in Europe, home ownership had never been remotely possible. Many found the older houses in Sydney and Melbourne affordable and with their strong family, language and community ties, especially among the Italians and Greeks, they preferred to settle in the one area. The Italian community tended to congregate in Carlton in Melbourne and Paddington and Leichhardt in Sydney. Immigration from Greece increased in the early 1960s. In Sydney the Greeks tended to settle in Newtown and in Melbourne, Fitzroy, Collingwood and Richmond. The new settlers did not spare themselves hard work and sacrifice, often to the disdain or mockery of native born Australians. Thus, many of them were able to purchase and quickly pay off cheaper houses in the inner city. Owner-occupied houses in these once despised areas increased spectacularly, and the fact that they were not levelled by bulldozers and replaced by high-rise flats as planned is probably due to

the new arrivals adapting so quickly to the entrenched Australian obsession with buying houses. Their Victorian houses were reroofed and protected from further decay and many went through another bizarre stage of their lives, a 'Mediterranean period' when their drab exteriors were painted in exuberant rainbow colours. Having been abandoned by the middle classes after their fall from fashion, despised during their dilapidation, the city terraces were now scoffed at by their critics for their new garish Mediterranean colours.

Attitudes to inner city living began to change in the early 1960s with a growing disenchantment and reaction to suburbia and the increased attractions of entertainment and white collar job opportunities in the central city. Young homeseekers started to buy terrace houses in Paddington and later Balmain in Sydney, and in Melbourne's Carlton and Parkville. Some of the southern European migrants were pleased to sell their terraces at a comfortable profit and move to an outer suburb to enjoy something quite

Overlapping circles give an effect of continuity.

Above left A registered NSW pattern, *NSW 170*, at 431 Riley Street, Surry Hills.

Below left A staid Adelaide pattern.

Above, an over-elaborate design of the 1890s.

Right A familiar Victorian pattern in St Vincent Place, Albert Park, Melbourne.

unknown in crowded European cities—their own garden. Young people who had perhaps grown up in suburbia were just as eager to escape it and move to the inner city. Many of the old houses were found to be remarkably solid and their new owners were delighted to find a lovely marble fireplace hidden behind wood and wallpaper or a cedar staircase and skirting boards beneath seventy years of paint and grime. Local councils and real estate agents were at first bemused by these early efforts at renovation and restoration.

The *Sydney Morning Herald* had an article on 18 September 1958 which asked 'cast iron—have you noticed?—seems to be making rather a comeback'. It was available in junkyards, the *SMH* noted, at one shilling and threepence a pound and it was becoming popular to use a panel as a summer firescreen or as a garden trellis. '"Quite a few people ask me to get panels for them and incorporate it in the design of their house," says architect Mr Morton Herman.' A few houses at this time had their iron

Australia's Iron Lace

Top right This extraordinary design has only been seen once—on a balcony above a shop in Mary Street, Gympie, in Queensland. The British lion and the harp of Erin on the narrow balusters are stridently nationalistic. The moustachioed grotesque mask with its sprouting foliage, the birds and fruit are familiar in Victorian pattern books which in turn were copied from ornament of the Renaissance: see page 248.

Below right This panel seen in Windsor Street, Paddington has many of the motifs popular in Victorian ornament. Arum lilies and fuchsias grow from a wicker covered pot which is suspended from a rustic frame. Birds are perched on the lower tendrils and vines are entwined around the frame. Stripping back such a panel often reveals the different elements to have been originally painted in different colours—usually dark rich reds, muddy browns and greens.

Opposite The new owners of Balmoral, an 1876 guest house in Katoomba New South Wales, were lucky enough to find an old tinted postcard of the building which enabled them to restore it to its 1890s colour scheme. This included picking out some of the floral motifs in the iron work.

The floral, human and bird motifs in this frieze from a Renaissance church door in Bologna often appear in late Victorian pattern books and are echoed in the panels shown on page 142.

lace freshly painted and the effect, the writer considered, was 'quaint' and had an 'incongruous elegance'.

The disillusion with suburbia sharpened during the sixties and the move back to the inner city turned into a rush to buy the once condemned terraces in suburbs which had now undergone a dramatic reversal of social status. Real estate agents were anxious to see houses change hands as many times as possible and gave a lot of publicity to the steeply rising values to attract investors and speculators into the market as well as home buyers. When the stock of houses in one area had undergone gentrification, agents opened offices in other old suburbs to attract attention to their potential and improve their popularity and so start another spiral in real estate values.

The 1960s saw houses renovated rather than restored. Many of the alterations to Victorian-era houses were unsympathetic and were carried out according to a passing fashionable whim—such as stripping the stucco render off external walls and the plaster from internal ones to expose the beautifully coloured, but highly porous, sandstock bricks. Feature walls and arches were built with the same bricks outside the houses and within. Home renovators during the sixties did not have the benefit of today's range of specialised publications on the subject, or reference to the research carried out by local societies and bodies such as the Commonwealth Government's Glebe Project. In the course of their rehabilitation many authentic features such as iron and wooden fencing, pavement and garden edging tiles and door knobs and knockers were removed, often because they were not recognised as being original.

It was soon realised that the exterior ironwork on an old house is often its most distinctive feature, and when a balcony has survived with its iron lace intact it adds to the merit and price of an unrestored terrace. Where the lace was missing it was replaced—reversing the 70 year trend of tearing it down.

Renaissance urns and flowers such as those found in this wood inlay design from the Palazzo Vecchio in Florence were also borrowed and rendered into iron: see pages 146 and 147.

The Renaissance urn and flowers was very popular in Victorian decoration. The design *above*, *NSW 200*, is common in Sydney, but another registered design, *NSW 236*, *right* has only been sighted once in William Street, Paddington.

With the advent of the 1970s Australians were taking a new pride in all things Australian and developing an avid interest in their colourful and varied architectural heritage. It has often been the public outcry against a mindless demolition or a brutal and unsympathetic development by councils and developers that has led to government intervention in preserving a building or an area. Australian government bodies do not have a reputation for innovative legislation in protecting the national estate—the legislation invariably follows an expression of indignant public opinion. Unlike France, Britain and the United States, Australia has no extensive system of grants to assist individuals restore their old or historic houses, nor is there adequate legislation to prevent the violation of buildings at whim. The millions of dollars that have been spent restoring the architectural heritage of the inner city houses of Australia have come mostly from the owners themselves.

The design *above* is a variant of *NSW 200* shown opposite.

This panel is familiar in Melbourne.

The 1970s saw some gratifying changes in that regard. The gentrification of some working-class, low-income areas had led to many of the older residents being alienated and bewildered by the change. Pensioners and protected tenants often found that they could not afford to live in an area which was undergoing the Paddington example, nor could they afford to leave.

Sydney's Glebe was such an area, almost entirely 1890s in character and owned by the Church of England. Rents were low but maintenance was almost non-existent. Glebe's houses suffered from leaking roofs, bare wiring, clogged pipes and termite infestations, but as the church's submission to the Commission of Inquiry into Poverty pointed out in 1973:

> The Church has a problem in that it is not possible to renovate these premises on the rents now paid, and in any case the increased rent after renovation would be beyond the means of the present occupants.[25]

The palmette on a Greek vase and a Paddington balcony.

Wooden Florentine lyre-shaped baluster and an iron lace pattern frequently seen in Melbourne and Launceston.

FLORENCE. PAL. VECCHIO

These three patterns date from the 1870s. The style was predominantly simplistic containing more space than fill.

As the demand for novelty increased during the 1880s and 1890s, designs became lost and blurred in their own complexity.

The Greek stele in the form of an akroter is from Myer's *Handbook of Ornament* 1888, and is easily identified in an Adelaide pattern above.

The Church of England had received this area and other lands in Sydney in free colonial land grants and was getting a bad press for its heavy handed treatment of protected tenants in preparing some of its properties in Bondi Junction for sale and development. In late 1974 the federal Labor Government purchased the Glebe estate from the church for 17.5 million dollars and, in a unique alternative approach to housing, avoided the displacement of the long term residents and added to the beauty and history of Sydney by a large scale renovation and restoration of the area. The Glebe Project also generated new and useful information on the technical aspects of housing renewal.

There has been a worldwide revival of interest in Victorian architecture, especially in cities which underwent rapid expansion during that era. San Francisco's 60 000 Victorian-era redwood houses are without

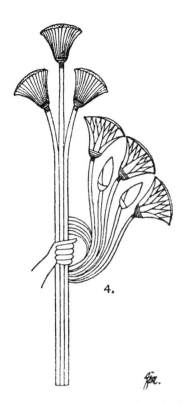

Stylised Egyptian papyrus and lotus buds, also from Myer's 1888 *Handbook*, are echoed in a registered Sydney pattern *NSW 322*.

iron lace but adorned with closely fretworked wooden motifs of foliage and sunrises and their parapets topped with Queen Anne 'witches' hat' towers. San Franciscans have painted them in glossy psychedelic colours of sunbursts and flowers, and patriotic eagles clasping crossed marijuana branches in their claws.

Guidelines for restoration

Owners of terraces in Australian cities have tended to use white or pale pastel shades when those colours were fashionable, but recently there has been a move back to the colour schemes used in the Victorian period. Research and the study of old photographs reveal a more vigorous use of colour than popularly imagined—exterior colours ranged from cream to

Above Restored terraces in Sydney's Glebe Project.

ochre and a dark rich ox-blood. Architectural details on the walls and parapet were in lighter and darker contrasting colours and the corrugated iron canopies of balconies and verandahs were often painted in alternate sheets or in broad stripes, often in colours used elsewhere on the building. The use of colour on the iron lace in the latter half of the nineteenth century is one of the most overlooked features of its history and restoration. Colours used were mostly dark but old photographs, although black and white, show the graduations of colour, though not the colours themselves. The late cast iron designs of the 1880–1890 boom period, in a frantic search for novelty, complicated their patterns to the point where outline and surface details practically disappeared. The picking-out of details was adopted to avoid this and to animate elements which flowed from pattern to pattern, or to bring out elements which would be otherwise lost. Stripping back a panel will sometimes reveal a floral element to have been picked out in a bright colour, but most were dark colours often matching the joinery. Rows of terraces built as one usually carried the same iron work pattern and were painted as one.

Once a commitment to the restoration of a Victorian house is undertaken, replacing or restoring the ironwork is one of the most gratifying tasks. The ironwork is usually the dominant feature of a facade and its rehabilitation immediately refreshes the character of the house.

With the new interest in housing restoration, new service industries have sprung up with specialised skills in restoration and in manufacturing reproductions of antique fittings. Every capital city has dealers who pur-

Painting this sweep of Paddington terraces plain white, though not traditional, has added to their harmony.

Woolloomooloo. Note the broad stripes on the balcony roofs. 'Rows of terraces built as one usually carried the same iron work pattern and were painted as one.'

Flora, the Roman goddess of springtime, as depicted in Botticelli's *La Primavera* (c. 1483, detail). The iron lace panel *right* was probably inspired by Flora, especially as its motifs include May Blossom, a flower usually associated with her worship. Note how picking out the figure in white animates the design. This balcony was photographed in Uralla, New South Wales.

chase old iron lace at demolition sites and also sell new aluminium reproductions. Most will undertake installations, offer services such as sandblasting and have connections with foundries who will reproduce castings from samples supplied.

Some Edwardian houses, especially in country centres were built with decorative ironwork, but where it was not originally present it should not be added.

Where the ironwork has been removed from a house and there are no old photographs available to establish its design, care should be taken to select a pattern contemporaneous with the house. If the house is a terrace, a reliable indication is the patterns which are repeated in the row or street. As we have seen in previous chapters, cast iron was a mass-produced item and patterns were chosen arbitrarily with little regard to individualism; custom-made designs, even in the most pretentious houses, were rare. If a terrace balcony has been enclosed the iron is sometimes still found within

Two very similar patterns using the bush 'flannel flower' as their central motif, however one panel is wider than the other.

the wood or asbestos-cement. Some regional differences may also be considerations—matching elements in the balustrade, frieze and brackets was a more common practice in Melbourne than in Sydney. The iron handrail was left bare in Sydney's balconies while throughout Victoria it is usually found with a wider wooden handrail laid upon it.

When installing panels with a flowing design, such as overlapping circles, or containing an upper or lower band designed to give unity to its length, the individual pieces should be installed carefully butted together.

If a panel is broken or missing it is essential to take an original sample with you when you go shopping for a replacement. Some panels may appear to be identical, but subtle variations were sometimes introduced and when the panels are separated from their row and compared it may be found that they have entirely different and unmatching contours. As cast iron panels are heavy and brittle they are very dangerous if dropped from a height and will crack easily. They should be handled as carefully as sheets

Above and right There are subtle differences between these two similar designs featuring lilies and daisies, notably in the contours of the arches and in the width of the columns. One panel cannot be used with the other variety as they also separate at different points.

Opposite Victorian developers often placed a corner shop, with a residence above it, at the end of a sweep of terraces. These are now often converted to restaurants or galleries, or as in this case in Sutherland Street, Paddington, into a spacious house.

of glass, and for safety and speed it is advisable to have two people on the job when installing or removing a balcony railing.

Where original panels are clogged and uneven with layers of thick paint and rust they should be given a *fine* sandblasting, preferably at a work shop that specialises in working with antique iron. A heavy or clumsy sandblasting can cause breakages, a fine one can 'bring up' a pattern and reveal detail otherwise unnoticed under years of hardened paint—try to pick the butterfly on page 160. Panels should be primed as soon as possible after sandblasting.

A sharp lateral blow or the steady pressure of a wisteria vine can break off a piece of cast iron. Broken pieces of antique iron can be brazed back together but, once again, only by a tradesman who is experienced in working with antique iron. There is always some risk that the change in temperature may cause a crack elsewhere in the piece.

If a small fragment of cast iron breaks off and gravity permits, it can be repaired *in situ* by using a modern epoxy cement such as Selley's Epoxy

Right A fine sandblasting revealed such carefully cast details as the birds' feathers (honey eaters?) and the butterfly in the upper right corner, which had disappeared from this panel under many layers of paint. The original paint work revealed that the berries had been painted red and the foliage green.

Above opposite These Paddington terrace balconies have similar elements in their panels but the central motifs differ.

Below opposite This picture of the balcony railing on the Lands Office in Armidale, New South Wales, illustrates the traditional method where the balusters fit into holes drilled in the floorboards and are unobtrusively fastened to the handrail with rivets. The same pattern can be seen in an early twentieth century photograph of Fremantle (page 128) where the painted flowers were picked out in different colours.

Repair Cement which sets in 3–5 hours on a warm day, dries white and accepts paint. If the breakage is in a difficult position and cannot be taped while the cement cures it can be wired to a backboard behind the panel. If, however, the broken piece is a large one and on a balcony situated over a footpath or patio area it should be taken down and brazed together. Modern iron or aluminium panels can be welded.

Some aluminium reproductions look so authentic when they are installed that one has to apply a magnet to them to establish whether or not they are iron. Others are so thin and the amount of metal in them so sparse they can be picked from a distance as being 'pseudo-antique' imitations—especially when installed in aluminium frames, which may be a quick and cheap method for a builder to employ but look hopelessly out of character in a nineteenth century building. They are often the only eye-jarring note in an otherwise harmonious restoration. Aluminium panels, provided they are honest reproductions, have the advantage of being easier to work with than iron and their lightness is an added advantage in cantilever balconies.

Some beautifully cast panels featuring Australian ferns and tree ferns appeared in the late 1880s and the 1890s. They are seen more frequently in Melbourne than elsewhere.

It is not possible to install original ironwork or aluminium reproductions unless the woodwork surrounds are level and sound. Brackets and fringes cannot be securely screwed on to wooden balcony beams or columns if they are badly weathered or rotted, nor can a balcony railing be levelled if the flooring it is to rest on is buckled or warped. A terrace size balustrade can be installed by a home handyman in the nineteenth century style without much difficulty.

Original baluster panels were sold with two 4 mm diameter holes drilled at the top of the panel where it comes in contact with the handrail and another two at the base where it rests on the wooden flooring of a balcony or the stone or cement of a verandah. These need to be drilled out if blocked. The lower holes received metal rods or spikes which fitted into matching holes drilled in the wooden flooring, preferably over the balcony's beam (note rods in place on panels on page 161). The task of fitting and fastening the handrail is made easier by sandwiching the levelled balusters upright between temporary wooden battens. The panels can then be

A Melbourne pattern of a tree fern bordered
by ivy and the ubiquitous shamrock.

A fern frieze and fringe at Albany Road,
Stanmore, Sydney.

fastened to the metal handrail by inserting rivets through holes drilled in the handrail to correspond with the two in the top of each panel, flattening the rivets on the handrail and then filing and polishing them flush.

In the case of concrete or stone flooring, the protruding rods or even the whole 'feet' of a panel were inserted in the floor into holes which were filled with molten lead. This is essential in erecting an iron palisade fence where the upright bars fit into a low masonry plinth which would eventually crack from the effects of corrosion and expansion of the iron without a lead buffer.

In restoring an old house, rehabilitation of the iron lace and the study of its design, more than any other task, gives a fascinating insight into Victorian attitudes and the taste of those who built and lived in the house during those years of confidence and overdressed pretension which seem so alien to us now. The patterns proudly displayed across the facades of mansions and lining the streets of working class terraces throw light on the

Nineteenth century cast iron decoration must have been a competitive business—prices for balcony panels were quoted on a per foot basis and some foundries were able to supply and fit specially cast odd sized end panels.

This modern aluminium reproduction is being installed in an aluminium frame which will immediately identify it as being pseudo-antique.

Unroofed balconies are rare. These two are in Quarry Street, Paddington.

cultural baggage of those who came to settle here. We can also trace the outlook of indigenous artists who looked at the distinctive texture of the native vegetation and fauna for inspiration.

We cannot say exactly what a colonial pattern maker had in mind as he carved a design in wood which was to be repeated in iron by a foundry, but we can see where the patterns were first suggested. Pattern books of ornament for craftsmen and designers were common during the nineteenth century and artists were encouraged not simply to copy but to improvise variations on the themes shown.

We have seen that Robert Adam's 1770s window guard pattern on London's Adelphi Terrace was included in Cottingham's *Director* (page 24) and found itself on the balconies of 1840s Sydney. Adam had adapted his pattern from the classical Greek anthemion and borrowed the thin flowing lines of its outline from the craft of the smith whose wrought iron swirls can be traced back to their source in medieval Europe. Other sparse and open early nineteenth-century patterns were imported to Sydney, Hobart and Launceston from England but most have disappeared. The sudden rise in wealth in Australia after the gold rushes and the scarcity and high cost of skilled labour made mass-produced cast iron attractive and accessible to all. But the Victorians' need for voluptuous ornamentation to reflect their new wealth had a profound effect on design and cast iron ceased being an affordable imitation of wrought iron. The opulence of the times demanded all of the cultural symbols of implied wealth and prosperity to satisfy the extravagant taste for ornament. Taking sides in the battle of the styles, between the disputing Classical versus Gothic factions,

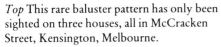

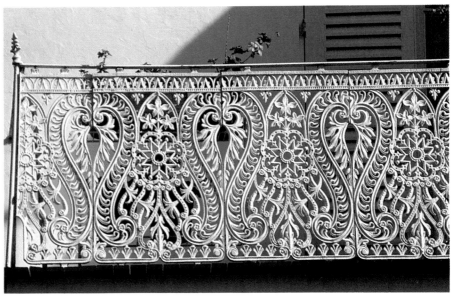

Top This rare baluster pattern has only been sighted on three houses, all in McCracken Street, Kensington, Melbourne.

Above right The tail of the lyrebird is thought to have inspired this baluster pattern.

Middle This bracket and frieze featuring the kookaburra was once a common sight in Prahran according to elderly residents but is now scarce.

Below The brackets portraying the sulphur-crested cockatoo can be seen in country towns and cities in New South Wales.

Transition. Iron work can be seen on some Edwardian houses, such as this one at Edgecliff, Sydney, before it was replaced by less ornate wood work. The motif on the fence panels is the anthemion—the same as that used on Sydney's earliest imported patterns.

craftsmen were able to peruse pattern books which supplied examples of Classical, Gothic and Renaissance ornament. The designs they adapted from these often ended with swirling tendrils, and with a nostalgic home-sick sniff for 'home', with roses, thistles and shamrocks growing from them. More stridently nationalistic and imperial symbols such as the British lion, the harp of Erin and the imperial crown also appeared.

Some designers turned to the Australian bush for inspiration and flannel flowers, the lyre bird's tail and ferns were reproduced in iron but often with the lingering nostalgia for the British Isles still in evidence; H. Sargeant & Co.'s kangaroo and emu bracket sprouts a tendril growing

Delicate crochet-like patterns such as the arching brackets on this building in Echuca, Victoria, are reminiscent of lacework and helped give rise to the expression 'iron lace'.

the shamrock, rose and thistle (page 86) and a Victorian registered design *Vic. 338* (page 164) of an Australian tree fern is bordered with ivy and the ubiquitous shamrock. The design with the most unmistakably Australian content of Aborigines, tree fern, kangaroo and emu, is, significantly, one of the rarest. Designers and pattern makers must have felt safer with familiar and conventional old world ornament, and, it must be admitted, gum trees, koalas and possums would have been difficult to outline or stylise in iron.

The late designs of the 1880–1890 building boom period show a complete abandonment of simplified taste, and design and elements were smothered in their own complexity. Changes in design from initial simplicity to lavish extravagance mirror the rise in wealth, and, by the same standard, the crash of the 1890s signals the beginning of the end.

Art Nouveau had its beginnings in a search for a new simplicity and it was from this source that a few early twentieth-century designs came, but its popularity did not spill over into decorative ironwork in Australia as it did in some European cities. So in about a hundred years cast iron decoration had come in a complete circle of taste and design, but in this case it was the symbol of the end and not a new beginning. Cast iron ornament was abandoned and has not been used since except for restoration.

'Iron lace' itself is a twentieth-century term, very subjective, romantic and non-technical—the foundries that made it during its heyday referred to it in their catalogues as 'iron railings'. The number of designs they made plus those which were imported would number well over a thousand and I have attempted to illustrate this book with a selection which expresses the historical development involved.

Above Art Nouveau made a rare appearance in wrought iron on this house at 9 Simpson Street, East Melbourne.

Right Cast iron Art Nouveau patterns can be seen on early twentieth century houses in Carlton, Victoria.

The buildings on which iron lace is found represent a vigorous phase of Australia's domestic architectural heritage and their popularity has also gone through the inevitable cycle of popular taste—government sponsored restoration schemes such as the Glebe and Woolloomooloo Projects in Sydney have displaced the Cumberland County Planning Scheme which urged full scale 'demolition and replacement'.

Australia's iron lace and the buildings which it adorns are a vital part of the growing excitement and pride Australians are taking in rediscovering their colourful architectural heritage. The inevitability of the cycles of decline and renewal and of fashion and taste has been acknowledged by writers from the Old Testament onwards. Few have been more explicit than the Victorian writer, Charles Eastlake, who commented in his *Hints on Household Taste* (1868), 'One of the conditions of aesthetic taste seems to be that in civilised life it shall revolve in cycles.'

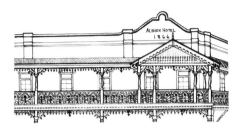

Catalogues

Space restricts the number of pages from surviving catalogues which can be reproduced here. Some catalogues, such as the "Sun" Foundry, run to over 100 pages. The sources of the catalogues mentioned in the text and reproduced here are given in the catalogue bibliography on page 189. These are examples of iron railings cast by John Crase & Co., Brisbane.

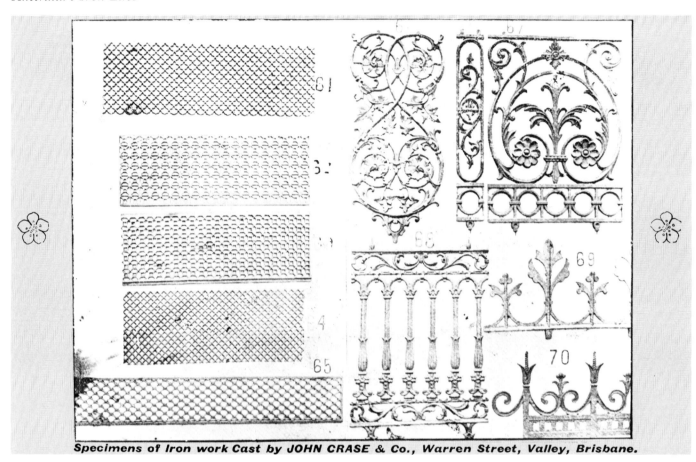

Specimens of Iron work Cast by JOHN CRASE & Co., Warren Street, Valley, Brisbane.

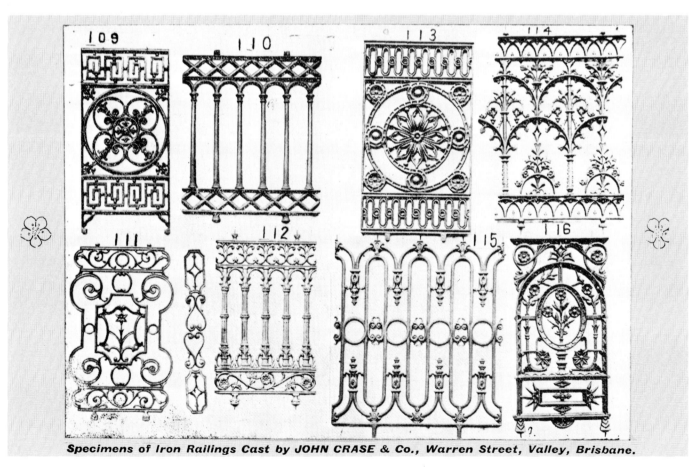

Specimens of Iron Railings Cast by JOHN CRASE & Co., Warren Street, Valley, Brisbane.

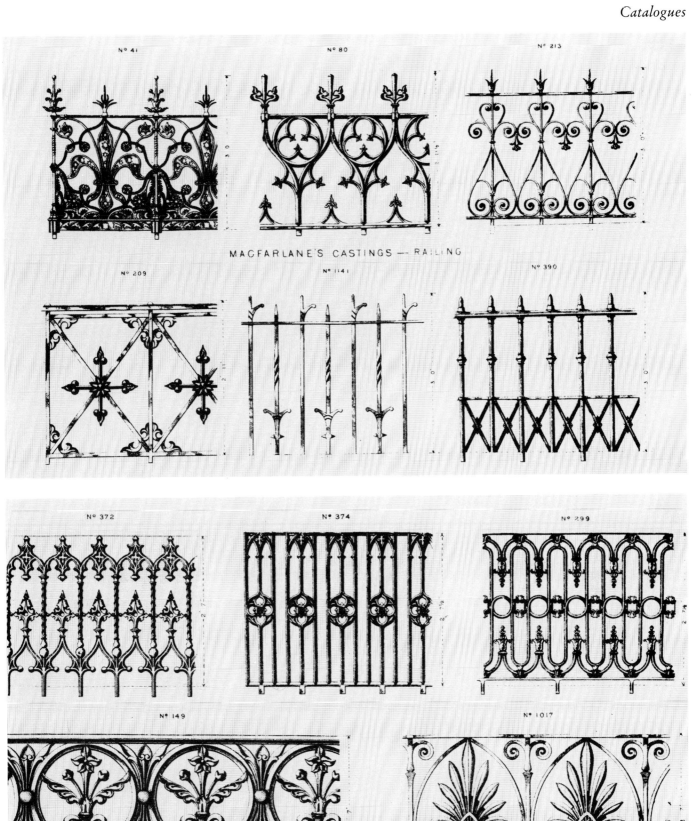

Nº 41 Nº 80 Nº 213

MACFARLANE'S CASTINGS — RAILING

Nº 209 Nº 1141 Nº 390

Nº 372 Nº 374 Nº 299

Nº 149 Nº 1017

1 FACE

For large centre ornament and standards, see page 274

SCALE

1 2 3 4 FEET

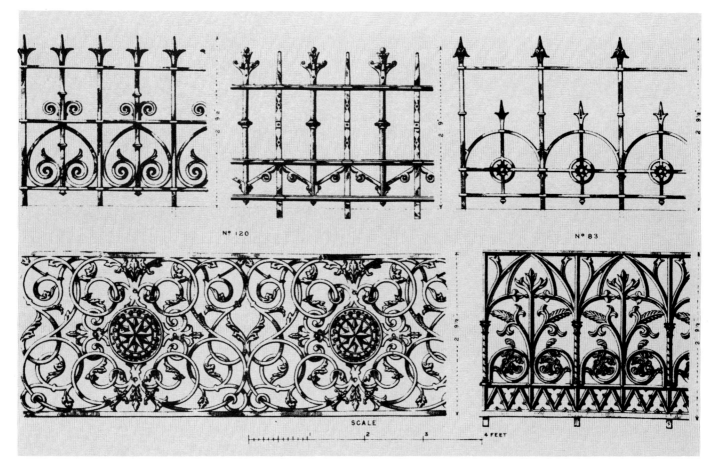

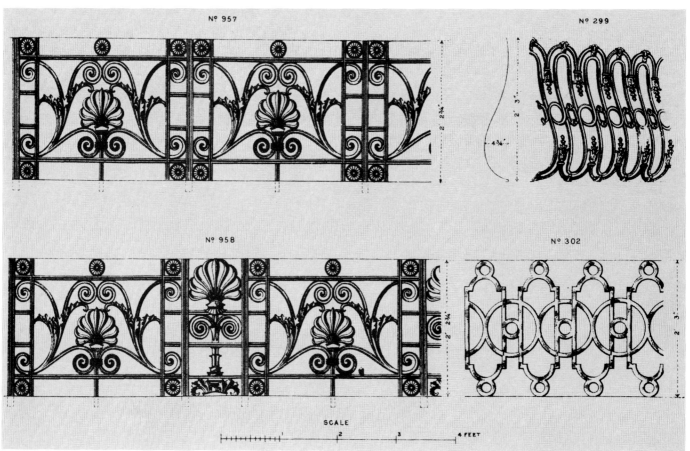

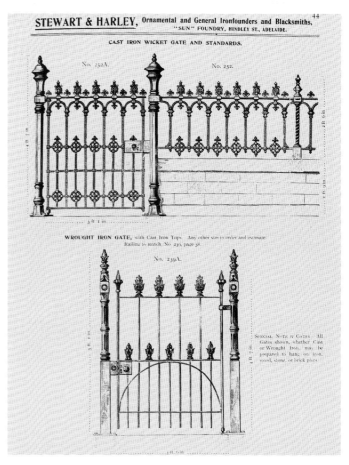

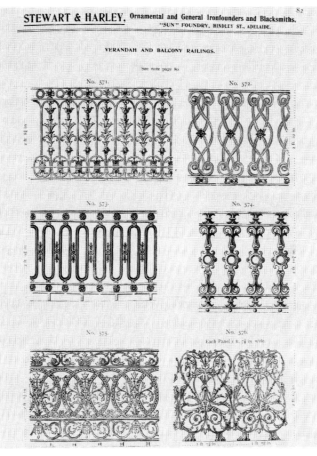

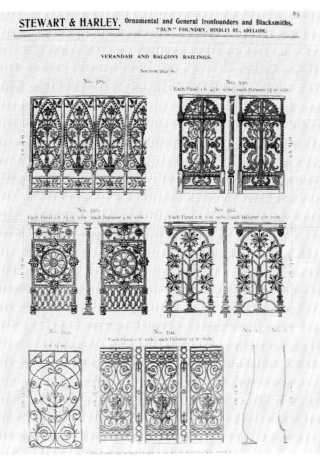

NSW 16

NSW 21

NSW 32

NSW 90

NSW 91

NSW 92

NSW 93

NSW 121

NSW 132

NSW 133

NSW 144

NSW 145

NSW 161

NSW 162

NSW 163

NSW 170

NSW 171

NSW 173

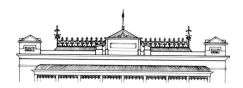

Registration
of Designs

When the manufacture of cast iron panels became a competitive business in the 1870s, foundries began registering their designs for their exclusive use. The date of registration of a pattern should not be used as a guide to date the construction of a building on which it is used. Some patterns may have been used prior to their registration and others were used for many years afterwards.

After federation the Commonwealth Designs Act became effective early in 1907 and the design registers of the states were incorporated in the commonwealth register and are now lodged in Canberra in the archives of the Department of Science and Technology. However, they are now copied onto microfiche (on Industrial Design Class 25–02) and can be viewed on request at any sub-office of Patents, Trademarks and Design of the Department of Science and Technology in every capital city.

In all, 77 foundries registered close to 350 designs, but this includes many cases where the same design was registered in several states. Many of the photographs and drawings were made over a 100 years ago and many have faded and are now unsuitable for clear reproduction. A large number of the designs registered were for tomb railings, roof guttering and ventilator grilles which are not the subject of this book and in some cases the illustrations are missing. What follows is a representative selection of registered designs, some of which are frequently seen, while others are extremely rare and may have been sighted only once or twice. The photographs are clear enough to facilitate identification, the numbers are those allocated at the time of registration, plus the date of registration and the name of the applicant.

Probably double the number of unregistered patterns was manufactured and, generally, unregistered patterns (sometimes variants of registered ones) are the most frequently seen.

By the turn of the century, through the lapse of copyright or negotiated purchase, surviving catalogues advertise registered patterns from various foundries. The 1897 catalogue of the 'Sun' Foundry in Adelaide has patterns which were registered in New South Wales and Victoria as well as some from the Saracen Foundry in Glasgow.

New South Wales registrations

Registration of designs in New South Wales commenced nine years later than in Victoria, the first registration being recorded on 17 December 1879. This was

NSW 180

NSW 181

NSW 182

NSW 184

NSW 191

NSW 194

NSW 202

NSW 200

NSW 205

NSW 210

NSW 217

NSW 221

NSW 236

NSW 252

NSW 273

NSW 298

NSW 15, 'a cast iron pilaster' but the illustration is now too faint to be recognisable. The same applicant, D. Livingstone, also registered a gothic-like baluster panel, *NSW 16*, on the same day. Seventy-five designs were lodged by 23 foundries. Some New South Wales registered designs are extremely rare—*NSW 162* has been identified only once, on a pair of terraces in Napier Street, Paddington. It is probable that a lot of Sydney's designs may have come from Melbourne during the 1870s—one of the most common patterns in Sydney is, in fact, a Victorian design of overlapping circles, *Vic. 70*, registered on 22 August 1872 by Cross and Laughton.

16	17.12.1879, D. Livingstone
21	4.3.1880, G. Fletcher & Son
32	18.5.1880, D. & R. Bradford
90	16.8.1881, Fletcher, Bennett & Frew
91	16.8.1881, Fletcher, Bennett & Frew
92	16.8.1881, Fletcher, Bennett & Frew
93	16.8.1881, Fletcher, Bennett & Frew
121	10.11.1882, J. & H. Juleff
132	6.9.1883, A. T. Rees & Co.
133	6.9.1883, A. T. Rees & Co.
144	24.4.1884, D. & R. Bradford
145	16.5.1884, J. Crase
161	3.9.1884, A. H. Brown
162	12.9.1884, W. Stephens & J. Bromwich
163	12.9.1884, W. Stephens & J. Bromwich
170	3.11.1884, A. H. Brown
171	11.11.1884, J. Simpson
173	n.d., Brown & Brown
180	3.12.1884, D. & R. Bradford
181	3.12.1884, D. & R. Bradford
182	4.12.1884, A. T. Rees & Co.
184	15.12.1884, A. T. Rees & Co.
191	8.1.1885, A. H. Brown
194	6.2.1885, A. H. Brown
200	25.3.1885, J. Simpson
202	8.5.1885, Swinnerton & Frew
205	15.5.1885, J. & H. Juleff
210	31.7.1885, A. H. Brown
217	23.10.1885, Swinnerton & Frew
221	2.11.1885, A. T. Rees & Co.
236	2.6.1886, Vann, Barrington & Co.
252	4.11.1886, W. L. Dash & Co.
273	25.7.1887, Dash & Wise
298	12.4.1888, Swinnerton & Frew
322	24.7.1890, J. J. Bromwich
350	18.11.1891, R. Gibson
352	22.1.1892, J. J. Bromwich
396	14.9.1885, J. J. Bromwich

Victorian registrations

Almost half of the 350 designs registered were done in Victoria by 49 manufacturers. The first design registered, a fringe and bracket of a nesting swan and her cygnets, was made on 8 April 1870, and is also one of the rarest. It has only been seen once on a house at 79 St Vincent Place, Albert Park, Melbourne.

4	8.4.1870, John Slater
7	11.4.1870, W. Hutchison

NSW 322

NSW 350

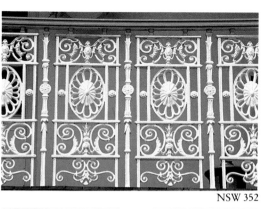

NSW 352

NSW 396

VIC 4

VIC 7

VIC 8

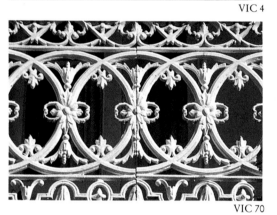

VIC 70

VIC 89

VIC 110

VIC 112

VIC 158

VIC 172

VIC 180

VIC 266

VIC 309

8   4.5.1870, J. Lyster & C. Cooke
70   22.8.1872, R. Cross & P. Laughton
89   7.5.1873, R. Godfrey
110   31.12.1873, W. Holland & A. Hutchison
112   31.12.1873, J. Lyster & C. Cooke
158   30.12.1875, W. Phillips, J. McWalter & H. Chambers
172   15.9.1876, A. Maclean
180   4.8.1877, A. Maclean
266   28.7.1880, A. Maclean
309   19.9.1882, A. Maclean
336   5.8.1884, J. Cochrane & G. Scott (fringe)
337   5.8.1884, J. Cochrane & G. Scott (frieze)
340   12.8.1884, J. Cochrane & G. Scott (bracket)
338   5.8.1884, J. Cochrane & G. Scott
341   22.8.1884, A. Maclean
371   20.1.1886, W. Thomson & S. Renwick (reproduction)
372   20.1.1886, W. Thomson & S. Renwick (reproduction)
444   17.11.1887, J. Cochrane & G. Scott
461   23.2.1888, G. Waterstrom (balustrade only)
465   12.4.1888, E. Walker & J. McC. Gray
634   7.4.1892, J. Cochrane & G. Scott
635   7.4.1892, J. Cochrane & G. Scott

Queensland registrations

Seventy-two designs were registered in Queensland by eight applicants; however, many were identical to the designs registered in New South Wales a few years earlier, and it is probable that during the 1880s the copyright could be purchased. Queensland's registered designs appear mainly in Brisbane, but on the shady verandahs of northern Queensland, in Townsville, Maryborough and Rockhampton there is a variety of unregistered patterns that are unique to their local area.

18   7.9.1886, H. Sargeant & Co.
19   7.9.1886, H. Sargeant & Co.
21   8.12.1886, W. G. Wilson (identical to *NSW 200*)
28   19.1.1887, A. Overend & Co. (identical to *NSW 194*)
30   19.1.1887, A. Overend & Co. (identical to *NSW 173*)
31   19.1.1887, A. Overend & Co.
38   19.1.1887, A. Overend & Co.
40   4.3.1887, J. Crase & W. Wilson (a rare Sydney pattern)
41   21.4.1887, J. Crase & Co. (registered by Crase in New South Wales, *NSW 145*, on 16.5.1884)
43   9.5.1887, H. Sargeant & Co.
44   9.5.1887, H. Sargeant & Co.
46   9.5.1887, H. Sargeant & Co.
51   16.6.1887, A. Overend & Co.
52   25.6.1887, A. Overend & Co. (identical to *NSW 170*)
83   7.2.1889, J. Crase & Co.

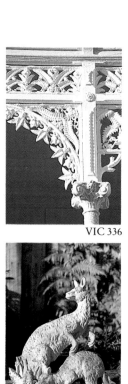

VIC 336

VIC 338

VIC 341

VIC 371

VIC 444

VIC 461

VIC 372

VIC 465

VIC 635

VIC 634

QLD 18

QLD 19

QLD 21

QLD 28

QLD 31

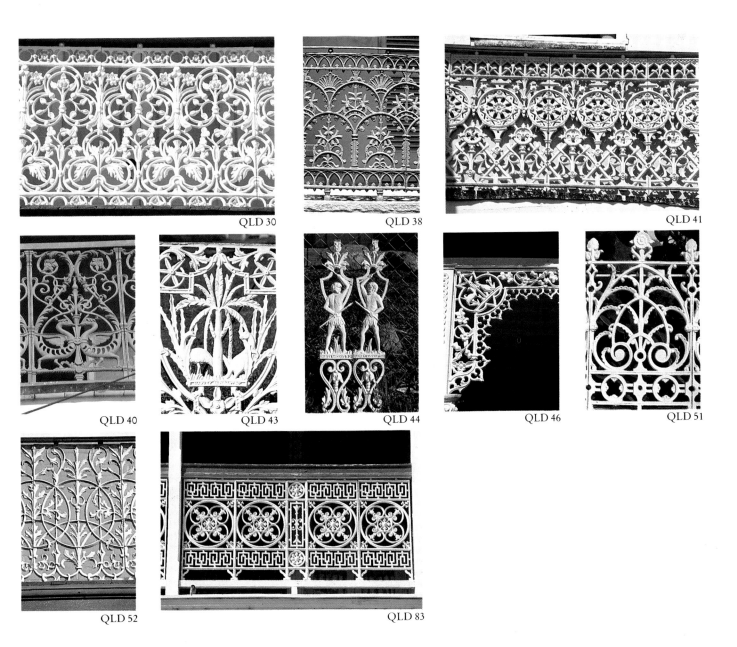

QLD 30

QLD 38

QLD 41

QLD 40

QLD 43

QLD 44

QLD 46

QLD 51

QLD 52

QLD 83

Glossary

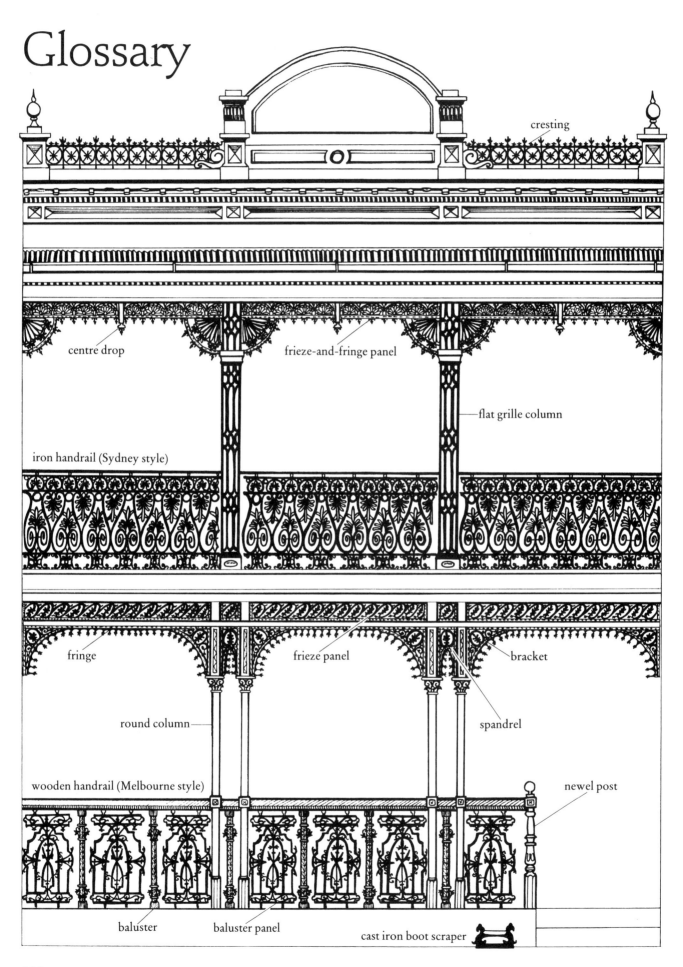

cresting

centre drop

frieze-and-fringe panel

flat grille column

iron handrail (Sydney style)

fringe

frieze panel

bracket

round column

spandrel

wooden handrail (Melbourne style)

newel post

baluster

baluster panel

cast iron boot scraper

Notes

1 J. Fowles *Sydney in 1848* annotated facsimile edn, Sydney: Ure Smith, 1962, Preface

2 L. N. Cottingham *The Ornamental Metal Workers Director* London, 1823, Preface

3 ibid.

4 J. Fowles *Sydney in 1848* annotated facsimile edn, Sydney: Ure Smith, 1962, p. 16

5 ibid. pp. 39–40

6 ibid. p. 50

7 R. Boyd *The Australian Ugliness* 2nd revised edn, Melbourne: Penguin Books, 1980, p. 52

8 J. M. Freeland *Architecture in Australia: A History* Melbourne: Penguin Books, 1972, p. 113

9 R. Boyd *The Australian Ugliness* 2nd revised edn, Melbourne: Penguin Books, 1980, p. 61

10 R. E. N. Twopeny *Town Life in Australia* London: Elliot Stock, 1883, p. 38

11 *The Bulletin* 18 November 1893, p. 5

12 'The Iron Foundries of Brisbane' *Queenslander* 20 May 1882

13 ibid.

14 ibid.

15 ibid.

16 J. Barlow as cited in M. Herman *The Architecture of Victorian Sydney* 2nd edn, Sydney: Angus & Robertson, 1964, p. 147

17 J. B. de Libra as cited in J. M. Freeland *Architecture in Australia: A History* Melbourne: Penguin Books, 1972, p. 194

18 Proceedings of the Engineers' Association of NSW, vol 8, 1892–1893, p. 37

19 J. Inglis *Our Australian Cousins* London: Macmillan, 1880, p. 147

20 H. Lawson *While the Billy Boils* Sydney: Angus & Robertson, 1896, p. 171

21 M. Kelly *Faces of the Street: William Street Sydney 1916* Paddington: Doak Press, 1982, p. 58

22 'Rabbit-O, Bottle-O, Pennies from Heaven: Hugo Street 1909' *Sydney Morning Herald* 23 January 1982, p. 40

23 Map, Cumberland County Planning Scheme, 1948

24 A. Harris *Settlers and Convicts* London: C. Cox, 1847, p. 17

25 Commission of Inquiry into Poverty Report, Canberra, 1975

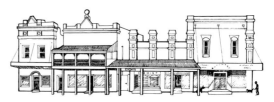

Bibliography

Baglin, Douglass and Moffitt, Peter *The Australian Verandah* Sydney: Ure Smith, 1976

Baglin, Douglass and Austin, Yvonne *Australian Pub Crawl* 2nd edn, Sydney: Child and Henry, 1980

Boyd, Robin *Australia's Home: Why Australians Built the Way They Did* 2nd edn, Melbourne: Penguin Books 1978

—— *The Australian Ugliness* 2nd revised edn, Melbourne: Penguin Books 1980

—— *The Walls Around Us* 2nd edn, revised by Trevor Howells, Melbourne: Angus and Robertson 1982

Briggs, Asa *Victorian Cities* Harmondsworth: Penguin Books 1968

Burden, Michael *Lost Adelaide* Melbourne: Oxford University Press 1983

Cannon, Michael *The Land Boomers* Melbourne: Melbourne University Press 1967

—— *Life in the Cities (Australia in the Victorian Age: 3)* Melbourne: Thomas Nelson 1978. Most popular histories of nineteenth century Australia concentrate on life in the bush, Michael Cannon gives life in Australian cities a candid and sometimes shocking scrutiny.

Casey, Maie et al *Early Melbourne Architecture 1840 to 1888* 3rd edn, Melbourne: Oxford University Press 1975. A delightful photographic record of Melbourne's early architecture. Many of the iron lace laden buildings have long since vanished.

Corbyn, Charles Adam *Sydney Revels of Bacchus, Cupid and Momus* edited by Cyril Pearl, Sydney: Ure Smith 1970. With a complete disregard for libel laws, Corbyn's court reports give us an irreverent and witty insight to Sydney in the 1850s. Present day politicians, police and magistrates must be thankful that the Sydney press corps does not have a writer with his gusto reporting on their follies today.

D'Allemagne, Henry René *Decorative Antique Ironwork: a Pictorial Treasury* New York: Dover Publications 1968

Department of Environment, Housing and Community Development *Urban Renewal* Canberra: Australian Government Publishing Service 1978

Department of Housing and Construction *Glebe Project* Canberra: Australian Government Publishing Service 1980. Contains the results of research into the use of colour on Victorian era terraces.

Evans, Ian *Restoring Old Houses* Melbourne: Macmillan Company of Australia 1979. Worth reading to plan an approach to restoring an old house.

Evans, Ian et al *Colour Schemes for Old Australian Houses* Sydney: The Flannel Flower Press, 1984

Fowles, Joseph *Sydney in 1848* annotated facsimile edition, Sydney: Ure Smith 1962. With superb engravings and delightfully pretentious prose, Fowles takes us on a tour of Sydney's dress circle, whereas Corbyn, a few years later, gives us an equally entertaining view of life in the stalls. One wonders whether they ever met.

Freeland, J. M. *Architecture in Australia: a History* Melbourne: Penguin Books 1972

Gloag, John and Bridgwater, Derek *A History of Cast Iron in Architecture* London: George Allen and Unwin Ltd 1948

Goldstein, Leona *A Study of Decorative Cast Ironwork in Paddington* Undergraduate thesis, Architectural Library, University of New South Wales 1984

Griesbach, C. B. *Historic Ornament: a Pictorial Archive* New York: Dover Publications 1975

Harrison, J. N. D. *The National Trust in Tasmania* Sydney: Cassell 1980

Hogan, Janet *Historic Homes of Brisbane: a Selection* Brisbane: National Trust of Queensland 1979

Howe, Renate *Slums and Suburbs: a Social History of Urbanisation* (Inquiring into Australian History series) Melbourne: Oxford University Press 1982

Kelly, Max *Faces of the Street: William Street Sydney 1916* Paddington: Doak Press 1982

—— *Paddock Full of Houses: Paddington 1840–1890* Paddington: Doak Press 1978

Larkins, John and Muir, Don *Victorian Country Pubs* Adelaide: Rigby Publishers Ltd 1980

Meyer, Franz Sales *Handbook of Ornament* facsimile edition, New York: Dover Publications 1957. Meyer's lavishly illustrated book must have been used extensively in the late nineteenth century as it rapidly went through successive editions. Originally published in German, the English translation of some words should be treated cautiously.

Molyneux, Ian *Looking Around Perth: a Guide to the Architecture of Perth and Surrounding Towns* East Fremantle: Wescolour Press 1981

Park, Ruth *The Harp in the South* Melbourne: Penguin Books re-issued 1975

Reader's Digest *Book of Historic Australian Towns* Sydney: Reader's Digest Services 1982

Robertson, E. Graeme *Adelaide Lace* Adelaide: Rigby Ltd 1973

—— *Ornamental Cast Iron in Melbourne* London: Routledge and Kegan Paul 1967

—— *Sydney Lace: Ornamental Cast Iron in Architecture in Sydney* Melbourne: Georgian House 1962

—— *Victorian Heritage: Ornamental Cast Iron in Architecture* Melbourne: Georgian House 1960. No approach to the study of cast iron decoration can be made without reference to Dr Robertson's works. However, new evidence, such as Russell's *List of Goods*, has come to light to push the date of locally manufactured ironwork back to the 1830s —earlier than Dr Robertson had believed

Robertson, E. Graeme and Robertson, Joan *Cast Iron Decoration: a World Survey* Melbourne: Thames and Hudson 1977

Roe, Jill *Twentieth Century Sydney: Studies in Urban and Social History* Sydney: Hale and Iremonger 1980

Spearritt, Peter *Sydney Since the Twenties* Sydney: Hale and Iremonger 1978

Stapleton, Ian *How to Restore the Old Aussie House* Sydney: John Fairfax Marketing 1983. The sections on columns, verandahs, balconies and cast iron lace should be read before planning and restoration of ironwork.

Catalogues

The overseas and Australian catalogues referred to in the text are held in Australian libraries with the exception of the *Barbezat et Cie* catalogue which is held at the Bibliothèque Nationale, Paris.

John Crase & Co.'s *New Book of Designs of Ironwork* Warren Street, Brisbane: early 1900s, John Oxley Library, Brisbane

Fulton, G. E. & Co. *Illustrated Catalogue of Fulton's Castings* 2nd edn, Adelaide: 1887, The South Australian Collection, State Library of South Australia.

Harley, A. C. & Co. *'Sun' Foundry, Illustrated Catalogue* 2nd edn, Adelaide: 1914, The South Australian Collection, State Library of South Australia. For the 1897 1st edn referred to in the text see under Stewart & Harley.

Macfarlane, Walter & Co., Saracen Foundry, Possilpark, Glasgow *Illustrated Catalogue of Macfarlane's Castings* Vols 1 and 2, 6th edn, Glasgow: n.d. Library of New South Wales.

Russell, R. *Hobart Town Foundery and Smithery, List of Goods* Hobart: 1835 (or earlier), Allport Library and Museum of Fine Arts, Hobart

Stewart & Harley *'Sun' Foundry, Illustrated Catalogue* 1st edn, Adelaide: 1897, South Australian Collection, State Library of South Australia

Stephens, William *Excelsior Foundry, Illustrated Catalogue* South Melbourne: 1901, School of Architecture Library, University of Melbourne

Directory

This list is an indication to the specialist services available in new castings, aluminium reproductions and dealers in antique ironwork. Inclusion does not constitute an endorsement of the organisation, nor is an exclusion meant to be a criticism.

In my dealings with specialists in decorative ironwork I have invariably found them to be generous and helpful with advice, and if any were unable to offer a service or a particular pattern they were willing to recommend another who could.

Ace Wrought Iron:
    330 Burwood Road, Hawthorn, Vic (03)818 4517
Australian Metal Moulders:
    22 Thomas Street, West End, Qld (07)44 6971
Colonial Lace:
    216 Brighton Road, Somerton Park, SA (08)295 1743
Cox and Rizzetti:
    86 Johnston Street, Collingwood, Vic. (03)417 3420
Delton Industries:
    160 Musgrave Road, Coopers Plains, Qld (07)227 2388

Ellery Castings:
    55 Drayton Street, Bowden, SA (08)46 1361
Furphy, J. and Sons:
    New Dookie Road, Shepparton, Vic. (058)21 2422
Grahame's Foundry:
    corner Liberty and Bedford Streets, Newtown, NSW (02)51 2938
Hanks and Lindsay:
    615 Hammond Avenue, Wagga, NSW (069)21 3387. This foundry will supply an illustrated catalogue.
Johnson and Wells:
    5 Gladstone Street, Hobart, Tas (002)23 5422
Luke, R. W.:
    5 Cardwell Street, Ballarat, Vic (053)34 1160
McMillan and Co Foundry:
    122 Edward Street, Brunswick, Vic (03)380 4594
Nielsen's Foundry:
    58 Gillan Street, Norman Park, Qld (07)399 5355
Pont, J. T. and Co:
    18 Gardiner Road, Rutherford, Maitland, NSW (049)32 7449
Priest, A. J. and Co:
    222 Planet Street, Welshpool, WA (09)361 2439
Richmond Ironworks:
    3 Paget Street, Richmond, NSW (045)78 2640
Terrace House Factory:
    corner Harris and Allen Streets, Ultimo, NSW (02)660 6768
Westside Manufacturing:
    372 Flindon Road, Kidman Park, SA (08)356 4206

Index